SEASONS OF THE DIVINE

SEASONS OF THE DIVINE

Written by
ARUN GUPTO

Photographs by
RENUKA KHATIWADA

RUPA

Published by
Rupa Publications India Pvt. Ltd 2024
7/16, Ansari Road, Daryaganj
New Delhi 110002, India

Sales centres:
Bengaluru Chennai
Hyderabad Jaipur Kathmandu
Kolkata Mumbai Prayagraj

Copyright © Arun Gupta 2024

The views and opinions expressed in this book are the author's own and the facts are as reported by him which have been verified to the extent possible, and the publishers are not in any way liable for the same.

All rights reserved.
No part of this publication may be reproduced, transmitted, or stored in a retrieval system, in any form or by any means, electronic, mechanical, photocopying, recording or otherwise, without the prior permission of the publisher.

P-ISBN: 978-93-6156-5229-9
E-ISBN: 978-93-6156-994-4

First impression 2024

10 9 8 7 6 5 4 3 2 1

The moral right of the author has been asserted.

Printed in India

Design and Layout by Dongol Printers, Kathmandu
email: dongolprinters@gmail.com

This book is sold subject to the condition that it shall not, by way of trade or otherwise, be lent, resold, hired out, or otherwise circulated, without the publisher's prior consent, in any form of binding or cover other than that in which it is published.

ACKNOWLEDGEMENTS

The Kathmandu valley had been a ballad-tune in my imagination while studying in the Terai and in India. I came to Kathmandu and saw how nature, myth, and humans interact to make an art of the city. My book is indebted to the cities of the valley.

I am always thankful to my gurus Prof. Shreedhar Lohani for enriching my knowledge of art and philosophy, literature and literary theory and Prof. Abhi Subedi for interacting with me for decades on art and literature of the valley. They both are my best companions in academia.

Those who traveled with me during the making of the documentaries, for writing, and for engaging in indolence by watching art and culture of the city are the ones who inspire me to work. Along with Renuka Khatiwada, Salil Subedi, Abhas Rajopadhyaya, Rajan Phelu also have been my co-walkers at times. Their enthusiasm to work with me are exemplary. Mr. Madhab Maharjan has always encouraged me to write books; I thank him for guiding me through the world of publication.

My family from parents to grand daughters provide best education to me. Some read with me, some edit, some provide professional advice, some walk past smilingly. They help so that I write. My grand daughter, Nieva has promised to write books like me and I think Anya will be inspired by her elder sister.

For

Prof. Syed Manzoorul Islam
(Manzoor-da)

PREFACE

Myth has been the most profound space for me as a teacher and researcher. Myth evokes poetry making sensibility, myth is allegorical, agrarian, it is innocent. But religion for me is institutional, coded, and dogmatic. Myth helps me conceptualize ideas to understand the art of the city, art in general. Myth thus is cognitive, which does not force you to believe something in absolutist way, you can accept and reject ideas.

My research in the field of myth and art has three fold experiences. I walk, make documentaries, and offer courses. Walking is cognitive knowledge with body in motion, making documentaries is visualizing and then retrospecting in quietude, and offering courses is finding spaces to discourse with students.

Divine is an idea. It is the myth of the highest order, which encompasses the beautiful and the grotesque, demonic and godly when the double bind seeps in to shape thinking. The divine cannot exist if the profane and sacred are decoupled. The divinity of knowledge is the divinity of sexual body, of sublime as the terror of nature. The idea of the city of Kathmandu is attributed by such double binds spread in the seasons. Our work has found more than four and more than six seasons. The chilly wind of dark nights in the forest hill emits the smell of summer flowers; the deep opening of the clouds in the rainy days sensualizes ingenuous shivering in the body. Season is an idea.

I am a theorist by training. I cannot make documentaries and write academic books without Literary Theory as the most potent notable, perspective, and explanatory convocation of ideas. If you cannot theorize, you cannot globalize, Prof. Ashish Nandy once told me. Gayatri Chakravorty Spivak writes: "... the production of theory is also a practice, the opposition between abstract "pure" theory and concrete "applied" practice is too quick and easy" (*A Critique of Postcolonial Reason*). The book is a theoretical practice on the cities of the valley.

CONTENT

Acknowledgements	v
Preface	ix
INTRODUCTION	
Mythopoetic Imaginary and Half of the City	1
NAG PANCHAMI	
Newar Myth of Reconciliations	11
GAIJATRA	
Sadness, Satire, and Soul	19
JANMASTAMI	
Mythical Anatomy of the City	31
HARITALIKA TEEJ	
The Double Bind of Happiness	39
INDRA JATRA	
The Agrarian Negotiation	53
MAHADASHAMI	
The Mystic Smile in the act of Killing	61
TIHAR	
Animal and the Self Amidst the festival of the Lights	69
CHATH	
The Sun Worship	81
CONCLUSION	93
Epilogue	125
Bibliography of Work Cited	133
Index	137

INTRODUCTION
Mythopoetic Imaginary, the Half of the City[1]

The relationship of city and art establishes Kathmandu valley as an energetic potential to represent the myth in modern urbanism. Such potentials recur constantly as the people of the valley interact with deities with performances, communicate through arts, revere plants and animals and multiple natural objects, and celebrate the self with the community. Such interactions develop a system of thought

---

[1] The idea of the book *Seasons of the Divine* evolves out of my journey with Renuka Khatiwada during the festival times from summer to early winter of 2019. She took the photographs of the people and their rituals with tirelessly critical eyes and I waited with notepads to write my ideas then and their and later elaborated and modified them. During these determined walks we accompanied more students while walking and shared their ideas with us. Abhash Rajopadhyaya explained the nuances of the festival times with his conceptual renderings, whenever he had time. We also talked to the locals, the adult and old gentlemen and women who spent their evening times drinking tea in the courtyards, shop keepers who told us stories of nature and supernatural, the artists who narrated the process of wood and metal carving related with the rituals. Renuka Khatiwada and I made the trips to captures images on various days and more particularly on the following date in 2019: Bhote Jatra: Jestha 26, Nag Panchami/Kalki Jayanti: Shaun 20, Gai Jatra: Shaun 31, Janmastami: Bhadra 6, Haritalike Teej: Bhadra 16, Indrajatra: Bhadra 27, Jitiya Parva: Asoj 5, Phoolpati-Mahadashami: Asoj 18-21, Kag Tihar/Dhanteras: Kartik 8, Laxmi Puja/Kukur, Tihar: Kartik 10, Maha Puja: Kartik 11, Gobardhan/Bhaitika/Kija Puja: Kartik 12, Chath: Kartik:16

The temple-shop in Kathmandu

by the interaction of humans with nature and supernatural. The energetic potential recur in mythopoetic imaginary: mythopoetic as poetry making ability of the culture and imaginary as the impact of the past in the present to continue comprehending myth of the past as renewed in the present. Myths always appear in the valley because the people have poetry making ability: they perform them when they walk in festivals and rituals, appreciate by making of sculptures and paintings, and create music and compose songs. Thus the myths manifest the potential within us as human beings.

The valley is the ability of the potential of myth. The Newars, the inhabitants of the valley, have internalized this relationship from thousands of years which are evident in the Mandala symbolism, in the temple complexes, around the stupas, lanes and market places, the Viharas, on the mountain tops and around the ponds. The myth and its potential is rare in modern urbanism.

There are thousands of modern urban spaces, smart cities, images of technology and development devoid of myth except those which are like Athens, Rome, and Baranasi; Kathmandu has its mythical voices visible to us all the time. Such visibility makes

Nature into Culture

the valley an exclusive urban space. The voices are multiple and varied as performances of songs and dances, rituals and theatres. We belief that we hear those voices when we spend a considerable part of our lives to listen to them with minimum of efforts. They come naturally to us like a leaf comes to a plant. One has to walk to listen to these voices. Like a leaf comes out gradually almost invisibly growing visible, the archetypes constantly are around us silently speaking, always growing with us. The city is the space of such mysterious invisibilities and silences. The half of the city is myth.

Modern urbanism, the rat race of competitive developments, blocks us from listening them and then we become the other half of the city, either devoid of myth or with the loss of myth. Being half is both conservation and loss which I will keep as my implied argument. When Sanjeev Upreti writes the novel *Hansa*, he makes effort to journey into the mythical half, the archetypal half with the narratives of people and animals, with ponds and its inner world to bring out a mythical-narrative consciousness as political consciousness. What he does is that he conceptualizes the ideas into narratives, he tells the concepts as narratives. *Hansa* is important for me for conceptualizing the inner working of ideas into stories. The mythical consciousness is embedded in a writer, myth is the structuring principal, we have known.

Approaches and Perspectives on Myth

With our engagement with the mythical orientation of the cities in the valley, the locals have come up with very open ended approaches to myth. The approaches define the sensibility of the people who live by myth in their various aspects of lives. The politics of religion in South Asia has brought a compelling conflict in the region where all that are mythical are historical, the characters and incidents from the *Puranas* and epics like *the Ramayana* and *the Mahabharata* have been historically factual to the extent that they have become the identity markers of religiously driven masses. One of the major approaches to myth has been grounding myth on history and reality followed by ensuing conflicts at present. The profundity of myth, at times, is forgotten as human unconscious projected in the dreams, as the potential to create arts and sciences, as the modes of telling stories, explaining realities, as engaging us in rituals, as knowledge of the world.

Arguably, we have observed that the myth is rarely taken as real to engage in the politics of hatred in the valley culture. Myth is always celebratory as performances. To make history of myth is rejecting the creative potential of human beings. I will discuss elsewhere how South Asia at present is reeling under the political efforts to prove Hindu mythology as histories. That is why Newar culture is open ended in artistic and philosophical senses. This is the half of the city which Kathmandu has preserved. Kathmandu conserves art and myth. It is not an exotic sangrila but a half space

INTRODUCTION

alike Benares, Athens, and Rome are, and there may be more, but rare and on the verge of extinction. The valley is not the sangrila of oriental imagination but a space which holds the impressions of the grandeur of art, the thematics of thought, the narratives of ancientness, the immediacy of the past, and the energy of myth in hundreds of *bahals*[2] and courtyards.

Kathmandu knows the divine not as powerful transcendental deities but as immanent beings near and dear to us, almost walking by your side, not visible but in sensibility, not visible but in the vision.

Myth is in contrast with the logic of science but such logic is not the sole base of human understanding about life around. Myth can be looked as the basic principle of our behavior. For instance, one may think about the shadow as mythical archetype. It is the dark side of human personality that appears and reappears and is reflected in our cultures. The shadow archetype Carl Jung[3] writes we store it as evil. And at the same time the shadow is, in fact, for Jung, neither good or bad, so it is innocent, the snake charges with its poison when it is in danger, the tiger kills the doe for survival, and humans also act in the similar ways. The shadow represents multiplicity. This is how the dancing devils-in mask performances- are also integral parts in Kathmandu imagery, they are dangerous but they protect too. The shadow turns dark, only when the innocence disappears and instead of internalizing the shadow which is innocence, the shadow becomes the sign of evil intentions.

---

[2] *Bahal* is a courtyard mostly seen in the traditional residential and religious premises.

[3] See Carl Jung. (1977 print) *The Archetypes and the Collective Unconscious* in *The Collected Works of C.. Jung*. Volume 9, Part 1. Ed. Sir Herbert Read et al. Trans. R. F. C. Hull. Princeton: Princeton UP.

Human behavior is always driven by this double bind of innocence and intention of harming the other or preserving the self.

Furthermore, human behavior is vast and myriad which cannot be comprehended by personal experiences only hence we need to know the art and literature of the cultures which we are not familiar with: they are the significant ways to know how cultures think and behave, and about their beliefs and attitudes. Reading other is reading ourselves in more critical ways because we compare, contrast, and find similarities.

Reading myths as Travelling Texts

Reading myths in this context is the same thing like understanding the inner potentialities in ourselves. The reading helps us explore our potentialities when we read other cultures. "Myth are clues to the spiritual potentialities of the human life" (Moyers: 1991: 16) Joseph Campbell explains to Bill Moyers. He tells:

> Read myths. They teach you that you can turn inward, and you begin to get the message of the symbols. Read other people's myths, not those of your own religion, because you tend to interpret your own religion in terms of facts – but if you read the other ones, you begin to get the message. (1991: 17)

The narrations of Canaanite, Yoruba, and Zulu traditions, creation tales of Jew, Christian and Islamic cultures, the stories of suffering of the Buddhists and Sikhs, they all add to our understanding as Hindus and Celts. Ethnocentric readings and understanding closes us from understanding the potentialities of the other.

Reading has become a political act in modern South Asia. One of my friends told me that Arabia was established by some Hindu sage named Ark. Such claims of religious nationalism do not only close the doors of reading the other but makes fun of cosmopolitan

INTRODUCTION

awareness that cultures and civilizations rose in variations. All the world is a Christian vision or is Hindu conceptual cosmologies is the problem of reading. The other side of the reading culture also is how not to claim that R. K. Narayan's *Guide* is an Indian novel, writes Spivak (*Aesthetics*: 2012: "Preface" 10). Claiming a text to my culture is a further instance of closing the potentialities of reading others. Like a novel does not belong to my culture, myths are not my texts. Myths did not develop out of cultural claims, they merely were responses to the vast phenomena of the world around. Such mythical responses are always travelling texts; they do not belong to me as a Buddhist or a Christian.

Reading the myths of the valley is travelling in the valleys of cultures. The myth of Kirtimukha does not originate in Hindu Kathmandu, or Medusa's not in Olympian Greece. The names are particularities but the ideas are universal. Myths do not have claims of origin and rootedness, they are neither universal nor local, they travel, crisscross amidst the vast unconscious of the species as humans. Like we cannot claim dreams as mine, myths are un-authored, un-rooted-nesses. In a metaphoric comprehension, neither Buddha was born in Kapilabastu nor Abraham belonged to the Canaanites. They are dreams of human unconscious always travelling like the spirits in the deserts and mountains, oceans and forests, villages and cities. When once we hold them to my culture and your culture, myths disappear and institutions of religion are born. If religion has myth as metaphors, even religions cannot be claimed as ours and their: they are further myths of human unconscious, but later constructed and given coded structures with closeted clams that in the beginning was the Hindu, Jews or Christian world view.

The Walk during the Season

Our walks in the cities, mingling in the festivals make us comprehend the archetypes and their energetic potential. We have gone through such readings while travelling in the cities and villages of the valley. The seasons of the divine, as the title of the book suggests, is the seasons of travelling by reading our culture as reading the other. I travelled with Renuka not only during the seasons of the festivals from August to November but many a times. For years I have walked with Professors Shreedhar Lohani and Abhi Subedi, and then with Salil Subedi, Pushpa Acharya, Archi Rimal, Bhusan Jha, Prabhat Humagain in particular. My walks with Soma Gupta had been a ritual for years. I have walked with my students as a regular habit for class assignments to observing events.

Walking is a multidimensional act from reading, writing, photographing; walking is revisiting the places, weaving layers of narratives in every revisitation; walking is experiencing the places with seasons with morning due, summer glaze, and silences of the night. Walking brings a strong sense of belonging as well as the apprehension of the unknown. Walking is always incomplete: you have to walk to 'the same place' but there is no sameness of the place when you revisit, it is different. Walking alone is confidence: Renuka

Death by Fire and Water (Pashupatinath, Kathmandu)

INTRODUCTION

The Face of the myth (A sadhu during Nag Panchami)

tells me how with a camera at hand, she finds her confidence as a woman, clicking photos while walking alone. Salil has walked in the valley streets while performing art while walking and I have followed him doing nothing but following him. I have waited in walking while Renuka clicked pictures for hours or Salil working but not talking for hours and still walking together. You do not make plans but decide to walk up in the mountains. Salil has offered to go on the brow of the hills, and Renuka and I followed him in tough trails. The performance around camera was a second thought after tiring walks for miles. In the remote corner of the globe, Amazon was burning and we paid tribute to the valley green hills by blowing music and performing art. The spirit of the forest, Salil may have thought, carried our melancholic message to the animals of the Amazon. Years ago, Abhi sir and I have performed with friends in the river, which became known as river stage. That was a walk to pay arts to the rivers of the city.

    The poetic acts of walk in and outside of the cities of the valley have made us realize that myth is the half of the city. Soma thinks

The Stupa amidst Urban Pillars

that walking is weaving a garland of past and present; if you do not walk, you cannot comprehend the city.

Thus walking has been a personal act of collective people. It is methodologically empirical research in the heart of the city in time. It is a geographer's exploration and a taxi driver's profession. It is the flâneur's loitering.

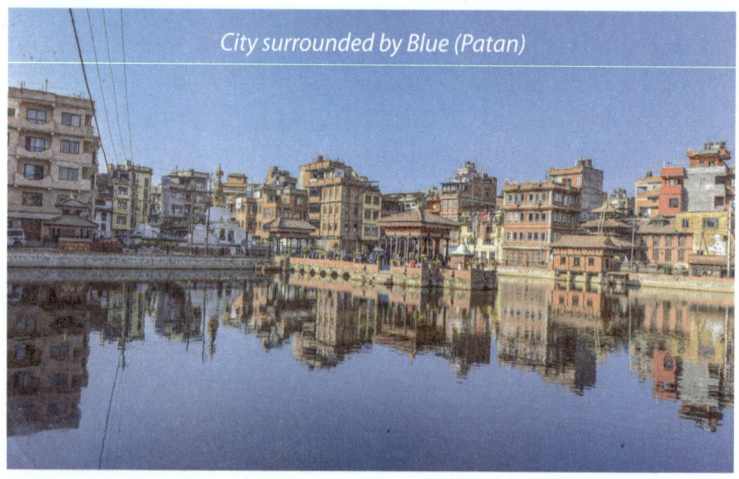

City surrounded by Blue (Patan)

NAG PANCHAMI
Newar Myth of Reconciliations

Naga image in Taudaha, Kirtipur

Snakes are the most ambivalent beings in myths and religion. They are the most powerful deities in Hindu traditions, both hostile and benevolent, feared and venerated. Nag Panchami is the festival of snake worship by Hindus in South Asia with the double bind of reverence and animosity.

Kathmandu narrative tradition reconciles and resolves the archetypal animosity between the snake and the bird, the Garuda,[1] found in Hindu mythical narrative tradition at large. The Newar narrative rewrites the broader Hindu mythology. According to many Hindu mythical stories Kadru and Vinata are sage Kasyapa's wives. Their rivalry to prove their sons' bravery took a conflicting competitive turn which ended in eternal animosity between Snakes, the sons and daughters of Kadru and bird Garuda, one of the sons of Vinata. The local version of the conflict is that of reconciliation.

According to Kathmandu popular myth Takshaka[2] is revengeful snake. He looses his abode when the valley waters dried out. He leaves home and in sinful revenge strikes people to death. Takshaka finally returned to perform penance but Garuda does not receive him well. Garuda captures Takshaka and then the battle between Takshaka and Garuda is resolved by the interference of Hindu god Machhindranath or Buddhist Lokeshwara[3]. This is a significant narrative account of resolution of the two enemies. Furthermore, Taudaha[4] pond in Kirtipur district of Kathmandu is the abode of Karkot naga. Karkot is prayed to bestow rain. The pond is on the southern eastern part of the valley.

Two of the tales are associated with pond and rain. The Newars of the valley are both artistic and agrarian people. They conceive agrarian awareness with environmental perspectives. The

---

[1] Garuda is a birdlike human in Hindu myths. He is also the vehicle of god Vishnu.

[2] Takshaka is a famous naga or mythical snake which has multiple narrative sources in South Asia. The naaga and Garuda is a local serpent living in Taudaha pond in the valley.

[3] Both Hindus and Buddhsits worship Macchindranāth, known as Bunga Dyah in Newari tradition and is incarnation of both Shiva and Avalokiteshvara. The temple of Macchindranath is in Patan

[4] *Ta* in Newari language is snake and *Daha* is a pond or lake.

vernacular aspect of the myth of resolution not only cuts across the grand narrative of mythical animosity but it also is a reconciliatory performance on the Puranic tales which have strong line of division between the two natural elements, the snake and the bird. Takshaka finally becoming the girdle of Garuda resolves the archetypal conflict.

"We do like such stories where conflict is resolved, we are peace loving people in the valley," a wandering sadhu told me when I asked him about how the enemies become friends. I had a conversation with him at a festival of Nagapanchami at Nag Pokhari in Kathmandu. Playing with the Puranic text and localizing it with the intention of reconciliation has been a marked psychological posture of the people of the city who are story tellers and who participate and perform the rituals at various seasons.

An artist in Bhaktapur could not draw sketches from the Mahabharata for the sculptures to give a concrete form of a deity. He told me that he needed time to psychologically prepare himself to the context of the epical conflict, intrigues, deceptions, killings in the stories. He was disturbed he told me and needed time to calm himself down before drawing sketches. Conflict has adverse effects on the collective psychology of the artistic world of the valley.

Many other reconciliations are evident in the valley art. In one of the valley sculptures Vishnu is on Garuda's back and a lion lifts them both on his, and on the top Lokeshvara sits. The narrative is manifested in the arts where the deities of two faiths are together: a Buddhist deity sits on the shoulder of Hindu god. The image is not that of a hierarchy but contains a double bind of privileging the one and at the same time supplementing the privileged. The 'privileged' holds the double bind of dynamism of being higher and being supported to be higher. There are many such images of performing the opposites in the valley art. One of the Swambhu chaityas reveal the similar play.

Such images of reconciliation are the cognitive variations of Basantapur Mahakal who puts his hand on the chest symbolizing the grotesque Bhairava as the deity of compassion. It is like the terrifying Kali entails motherhood. The understanding which such stories and arts contain represent the symmetry of yoga and the complexity of tantra. The tantra art is the manifestation of celebrating the grotesque which is un-Vedic and un-Brahmanistic in traditional sense because Vedic perspective at large considers the tantra as deviant. The tantra's artistic manifestation encompasses the serenity of Yoga consciousness in the arts: thus the opposites are placed in performative doubles. Neither tantra is impure and lower form of ritual and art nor yoga is pure by demeaning the tantra in such valley arts. The amalgamation of tantra and yoga minds reveal the psychological posture of the Newars. Holding the upper position is not the hierarchy of high and low. Such sensibility is evident in the arts in Hindu and Buddhist arts.

The pond, the lake, the water is the abode of the snakes in multiple valley narratives at Taudaha near Kirtipur, Sidha Pokhari in Bhaktapur, and Nag Pokhari in Kathmandu. Snake's association with water-world is akin to its abode with the nether world, the *patala*, the underworld. The nagas are the inhabitants of the underworld which possess the gems and precious stones, according to many myths as well as per our common understanding that the earth contains valuable. The underworld is the hidden of the nature, the life source in terms with whatever the earth bestows on humans, as the anthropomorphic worldview constructs. The water covers the preciousness within the earth and the snakes protect them by being threats to the intruders.

Water imagery is vital as the life source of valley civilization. Snake symbolism comes seemingly adversely with culture where they are considered as the elements of evil. The paradox is worth conceptualizing. Gopal Sing Nepali presents the characteristic of the valley in relation to the snakes:

NAG PANCHAMI

The Nagas are as popular as they are numerous. The[y] (sic) are believed to be the agents of rain and custodians of treasures. The name Nag-hrid Or Naga-vasa, the abode of serpents, given to the valley of Nepal in its traditional history, shows the predominance of snake-cult. It is believed that there are nine different Naga-gods of different colours in the valley. They are entrusted with different functions. (2015: 323)

The snake is symbolic to the psychology of the urban mind which is engrained in folk and agrarian culture. The more people believe in the myth of the animals and deities, the more people follow rituals holding constant fascination of the folk. Folk is always present; agrarian consciousness is perpetually visible in the city. This is a very immediate visuality of the valley culture which is always close to the folk.

The snake comes as a powerful symbol of the emotions of the people which is feared as well as venerated and taken as the harbinger of fertility and wealth. Furthermore, the abode of the snake is invisible, hidden, and mysterious. The underworld is the space where the serpents reside. These are from myths as narratives which communicate symbolism of the natural world.

The poetry-making ability of a culture speaks through symbols. Poets and artists have the ability to express such symbolism in creative expressions, the ability comes from the very space of the culture they belong to. All cultures are rich and all have symbols to understand the visible and invisible phenomena they are surrounded by. Symbolization is a natural human attitude which comes due to the being in the world. Max Bileu writes:

> Thus the creative experience engenders an attitude expressing the need that we all feel to become something 'other' than what we are, in other words to attain an unconfirmed state of autonomy, even if only for a few moments at a time. As

a consequence, a work produced in this particular state is not a simple play of the imagination or the expression of a real emotion, but rather an account of the sort of existential experience that myths are felt to represent. (1996: 863)

Once this attitude towards the symbolic value is misunderstood, cultures become incomprehensible. The reconciliation thus is the attitude to see animals as the very essence of the myths which is how the narratives present them as symbols of good and evil, protectors and destroyers and with many such characteristics. Carl Jung explains symbol and its signification:

> Thus a word or image is symbolic when it implies something more than its obvious and immediate meaning. It has a wider "unconscious" aspect that is never precisely defined or fully explained. Nor can one hope to define or explain it. As the mind explores the symbol, it is led to ideas that lie beyond the grasp of reason. (*Man*: 1964: 20-21)

The reconciliation also is the explanation of something not obvious to logic and reasoning. There are many tales of the snakes in the valley and their meanings are found at the level of transforming the object into symbolization or signification.

What has been striking in our travelling experience is that nature is brought close to us by the power of myth. Kathmandu, Kirtipur, Patan, Bhaktapur, Sankhu, Banepa and many other human abodes, the mythical half of the city is in a dire condition of failing to the challenges, both good and ugly aspects of urbanization. Walking in the nature in the valley is still possible but with difficulties. Kathmandu is, arguably, one of the rarest of the valley cities in the world where the mythical 'half' is still visible.

There are further creative images in myths and arts of the valley, the hoods range from five to thousands. Shesh or Ananta naaga (who makes a grand coiling as the resting bed for Vishnu) and Vasuki (as girdle of Shiva) and his sister Manasa are the most famed mythical serpents. Kaliya is the evil serpent on whose hood Lord Krishna danced and subdued. In the valley narratives Takshaka and Karkot are related with Taudaha pond. The serpents are pervasively around us through imagery and their symbols.

Note:
I have not included *Janai Purnima* or *Raksha Bandhan*, a festival which is celebrated a week or two after Nag Panchami. The festival of sacred thread is initiation to Brahmanistic Hindu fold. It is a festival of utmost discursive significance which needs more study.

The Snake Goddess

GAI JATRA
Sadness, Satire, and Soul

The sadness and the satire coalesce in the festival of Gai Jatra which falls in August-September every year. On the one hand, the family of the deceased ascertain that the soul of the dead goes heavenward, and on the other hand, the festival becomes the time of writing satire. The tragic and the comic, the bereavement and masquerading come together. The amusement related with death is not demeaning the tragic but an evolution, a community consciousness of in-betweenness as the emancipation through performance. The performance is enacted mythically by seeking solace for the dead, politically by writing satire on authority, and dramatically by masquerading the animal cow who is the divine rescuer.

The music of sadness

The somber

For the soul's journey

Gai Jatra, Gopal Singh Nepali writes:

> is known in Newari as *Sa-ya-wane-gu*. Sa means cow; *ya* represents jatra and *wane-gu* means "to go." It takes place on the first of the dark-half of *Bhadra* (Aug-Sept). The usual belief connected with it is that from the *Sithi Nakha* day (the 10th of the bright-half of *Jaistha*), the day when the worship of *Dewali* comes to an end, the gates of the kingdom of Yama are closed and, therefore, those who die after that date are unable to get admission to heaven. The festival of cow is, therefore, designed to help the dead soul to enter Yama's kingdom or heaven. As the belief runs, on the cow festival day, the cow is unable to thrust open on of the doors of Yama's with its horn, while the other door is believed to be open later on the *Vanra Jatra* day (the 13th of the dark-half of *Bhadra*. (2013: 353-354)

GAI JATRA

The impersonators of the cow are worshipped from each family and they later join the festival. The boys as the cow mask-wearers join the procession with the relatives of the dead. It turns to be a big procession as they march toward the center of the city: in Kathmandu, the central space is Basantpur (354). Nepali describes the regional variation of the festival[1] in Panga, Kirtipur, Charikot in north of the valley, and the city of Dhankuta in the eastern Nepal (355).

The cow has a significant hold on soul's transformation into a ghost[2] if the divine animal does not help the soul to reach to the heaven. The term for ghost in Nepali and other north Indian languages in *bhoot* and more appropriately *preta*. The transformation of the soul into *preta* is associated with sin. The cow has the power to purify the karmic deeds of immorality and sin if she is properly worshipped, the religious belief is.

The association of the sacred, the fear and reverence of the journey of the dead, the presence of the holy cow, and even the animal sacrifices are not grotesque to the devotees[3]. Grotesque is not binary of beauty – I have mentioned elsewhere, especially in relation to Durga and Kali rituals – but they merge in Hindu South Asian conceptualization. Instead of grotesque, it is the joy to perform something for the besieged relatives. The story of Prakash

---

[1] "The Buddhist Newar groups of Vanra, Udas, and Manandhar have no tradition of cow procession. Their part of the festival consists merely of going round the city, playing on their respective musical instruments," writes Nepali (354).

[2] Ghost in the Hindu religious vocabulary is *preta* suggesting a ghost who is perpetually hungry. Sinners, if not assisted by some blessing, assistance, and rituals, remain in the *preta*-world which is a space beyond physical and paradisiac world.

[3] My opinion about the rituals of sacrifice is complete denial though its symbolism in the ancient traditions is a matter of anthropological discourse.

Gai Jatra spectators, Bhaktapur

Malla's queen who had lost her son and was gripped with suffering, is the realization about the truth of death. The king had diverted the procession of Gai Jatra to pass by the palace so that his queen could witness masquerading boys with the masking and decorating themselves as cows and be happy. As the story goes, the queen gradually realized that death is inevitable. She was both pleased and went through a sense of awareness about life and death. The queen used to sit up on a pedestal while the crowd passed by. She smiled and people were happy, from the king to the public. The masquerading is not farcical but is purposeful. The cow is enacted as a rescuer. The mocking and laughter come only in the tradition of writing and performing satires. The evolution of satire is the parody with purpose.

Gai Jatra is a performance of joy to pave ways for the soul. The festival heals the pain with masquerading, masking, and walking with families and communities. There is a predominance of color white because the cow generally is fair. White is the color of sobriety in Hindu visuality. The cow is mother to the devotees. The mother carries to soul by swimming across the river Baitarani, the mythical river which exists in transcendental space.

GAI JATRA

Take us to the ultimate abode

The divinity does not descend as the avatar to rescue humanity from the evil, but the mother goddess floats upward from as the etheric divinity, not transcendental one, and takes wandering soul to transcendental realm. The role of the divine rescuer is performed upward, unlike many other gods and goddesses descending to the earth to bring peace to the world. She lifts the human abstract essence, the soul, from a wandering condition to an ultimate supernatural space. Gai Jatra symbolizes an exclusive moment of atonement or expiation both for the living and the dead.

In the midst of the performance, there is the *lakhe* who dances in frenzy. Why does the dancer in demonic shape appear in the festival? What does he achieve in this journey of expiation? Nepali writes about the jatra in Panga, Kirtipur, which displays different rituals in its details:

> In the evening again, they assemble at the central square to witness the *lakhe* dance. The Kusle priest sacrifices a hen to

Ganesh by wringing its neck. Then he jumps into the tank and the sacrificed hen is taken away by him... followed by distribution of a piece of buffalo skin to each group of the musicians. In addition, a piece of the sacrificed buffalo leg is given to the heads of the eight groups of musicians. As soon they receive the pieces of the skin and legs, they jump into the tank. The *lakhe* dancer is given the buffalo's head; but he does not leap into the tank. Instead he circumambulates. (2013: 356).

There is a striking difference in Brahmanistic Hindu tradition with the local. Ganesh is a god who is not worshipped with flesh offerings in majority of Ganapati (another popular name of Ganesh) rituals in India and also in Nepal. Like in Vaishnav tradition which worships Vishnu as a vegetarian deity, Ganesh also is a vegetarian deity. Such sacrificial ritual may be a matter of awe and shock to many devotees of Ganapati tradition of rituals. Goat sacrifice in Suryavinayak (Vinayak is yet another name of Ganesh), Bhaktapur, is performed during the festival. Along with such rituals of sacrifice to a god who belongs to a different characterization by dominant Hindu tradition, the bird and animal blood in his alter establishes an entirely contrasting ritual practice. Ganesh is the son of goddess Parvati and lord Shiva. Parvati narratives associate her with Durga. Hence Ganesh is not remote to the power cult of Durga who is a deity of war also and receives animal sacrifices as herself and also as Kali and many other similar goddesses. The ranked god Ganesh in Brahmanistic Hindu belief system has different characterization. Due to the dominance of tantra form of Hindu and Buddhist ritualism, Ganesh and many other gods are associated with animal sacrifice. Krishna, an avatar of Vishnu, gets flesh and blood as offerings during Krishna Janamastami festival.

Tantric ritualism is immediate as immanence, here and now, very local and thus contextual. The vegetarian ranked god of

Brahmanistic pantheon is also a ranked god of valley pantheon who is offered animal sacrifice. In such contexts, the presence of the *lakhe* celebrates the sense of the wild enthusiasm amidst sacrifices. The moral god is partial if divinity is conceived in the image of the human. God as a reflection of human traits cannot be devoid of human characteristic. The eulogy of man as perfection like angel and god is the most beautiful lying about human beings. Humanism has such symbolisms of lying. If the praise were not in the domain of literature, the teleological political human is 'both' sacred and profane, moral and immoral, good and bad and hence not conceived in binarism, that is, the sacred does not contradict the profane or dark contradicting the light. Tantra strikes at the binarism of ranked religious imagination by worshiping Ganesh with sacrificial rites, and also bringing the demon dancing while the cow is worshiped to rescue the soul. Wild enthusiasm needs the demon as the metaphor of primal celebration. Ganesh represents the celebrating human being with joy of life and rupture of rigid codes.

Furthermore, *lakhes* in the valley have diverse performances. *Gula lakhe* is not supposed to see the main *lakhe*, and the main *lakhe* is not supposed to come to *Dagi* or *Dagini*, a demon or the mother of god Indra (363). The extensive Hindu tradition in South Asia does not depend on Vedic and Puranic prescription only, it has it own ranks and positions. The king of the god, Indra has a demon mother and at the same time, the earth goddess Aditi too is his mother. Hindu ritualism, idolism, imagism, narrativism range in immense diversification.

The presence of the demon is as normal as the human and divine act together in the seasons of the divine in the valley. *Lakhe* are numerous in valley mythical conception. *Majipa lakhe* has a special place as protector children. He belongs to Ranjitkar Newar and is the chief dancer in Indra Jatra festival. Since he resides in the body of the girl, Majipa, who was in love with her and wanted

The mask of the demon

to marry her, he was imprisoned by daring to enter in the human world. He was bodied in her, and was given the task of protecting children by the king. There is demon or a body *Jhyalincha* who teases *Majipa* creating fanfare in dancing.

The demon's influence in Valley myth resembles Tibetan belief systems too. The demonic figures are protectors too, as we have seen. Rene de Nebesky-Wojkowitz writes,

> The group of protector and guardian deities, which comprises some of the best known gods and goddess of Tibetan-Buddhist pantheon, is considered to be divided into two main branches, firstly the powerful, high ranking deities, known as '*jig rten las 'das pa'i srung ma*, i.e. the gods and goddesses who have passed beyond the sixth spheres of existence; to this group belong, "all the protective deities of the eighth, ninth, and tenth

rank", as my Tibetan informants explained it. Secondly, those deities who are still residing within the spheres inhabited by animated beings and taking an active part in the religious life of Tibet, most of them assuming from time to time possession of mediums who act then as their mouthpieces. These gods and goddesses, known as the *'jig rten pa'i srung ma* or *'jig rten ma 'das pa'i srung ma*, are also frequently called *dregs pa*, "the haughty ones", an expression derived with a haughty fierce facial expression. (1996: 3-4)

The task of responsibility has been a significant characteristic of Hindu and Buddhist pantheonic traditions. Durga emits negative forces to tackle the demons and once the task is accomplished, these deities are further ranked as guardians, protectors, mother, and knowledge deities. There is no rigidity of identity in such supernatural performances. *Lakhe* is given the task of protection. Hariti, according to Buddhist myths was rescued by Gautama Buddha and she turned to be the protector of children whom she used to devour to quench her hunger.

The act of transformation is not a transformation from one state to another but the double is already with the self, the good resides in the demon, or the demon in the good. But the double has to be cultivated by the guru, king or the priest. One dies to let the other be born. The demon dies to transgress into the other. He or she moves from the immoral to the moral act of performance.

The king who forgave Majipa and gave him a new role did not transgress any moral code but forgave with the realization of the potential of a demon who if can fall in love must have the potential to perform more than what he possesses, the evil. The king was wise to delve into the potential with the act of forgiveness. He behaved like a thoughtful ruler. Forgiveness is forgiving the unforgivable, welcoming the unwelcomable[4]. Forgiving the demon must carry a severe consequence. Buddha had taken Hariti in his fold to transform her from a child-eating demon to a protector and similarly, Goddess Durga had taking the buffalo demon into her fold rather than killing the devil. I have analyzed Durga's act in such a term of forgiveness in the chapter "Mahadashami: The Mystic Smile in the act of Killing."

Why does a *lekhe* dance? What is the role of the dance in Gai Jatra? Does it fulfill some social purpose? Dance rituals and festivals have primarily been for amusement as distractions from diurnal activities, participation in social bonding, celebrating some causes and for many such expressions. Frances Rust analyses dance,

> The structural/functionalist approach consists, basically, of the assumption that every social system must solve certain functional problems (for if it did not, the system would disintegrate). Following the usage of recent theorists these problems might be termed" (1969: 2)

as "Pattern Management and Tension Maintenance, Adaptation, Societal Goals, and Integration (3). Regarding management and maintenance of tension, Frances Rust writes, "Pattern Management and Tension Maintenance," … "refers to 'socialization', (the process by which cultural patterns come to be incorporated in the personalities of members of the society) and to the 'management' of potentially disrupting emotional disturbances and distractions" (3). His analysis regarding social dance appropriates the approaches to dance. How then to theorize the functions of demon dance which is integrated in the social fabric from the myths of the supernatural?

---

[4] See Jacques Derrida. (1997). *On Cosmopolitanism and Forgiveness*. Trans. Mark Dooley & Michael Hughes. London: Routledge (17-18).

His second functional problem is "Adaptation," which "includes adaptation to the social and non-social environment, division of labour and role differentiation" (3). The key term is non-social environment for our context. Instead of discoursing the origin of demon dance, my purpose is to address the questions related with reason, role and purpose, which I have asked above.

In *lakhe* dance or in many such demon dances, the existence of the supernatural appears in patterns: the gods, demons to humans. The mythic complement the social by being supernatural to cultural. The reason thus may be multiple, ranging from faith in the supernatural to agree to the supernatural as modes of amusement. The grotesque complements the god or goddess as the other. The demon as the other to the god is familiar to human through dance. There are multilayered relationships of the human with the demon, as other to society, as other to the gods, and to humans. Along with such association, there are multiple emotional situations which connect human with the demon, from amusement to fear. Ironically the demon is not very other and probably the king is wise enough to realize it.

Gai Jatra, one of the initiating festivals of the season combines the sadness and joy along with satirical tradition. During the heydays of monarchy, even the kings dared not retort to such literary expressions.

JANMASTAMI
Mythical Anatomy of the City

The crowd below at the Patan Darbar square, around five in the evening was a spectacle of myth, folk, and history. The impression of a folk festival in the midst of the city brings a magical dynamism in space and time. The evening of Krishna Janmastami festival weaves a play: the flutes floating in the air mingling with the voices of the crowds, the celebration of the myth in the mytho-historical complex of the Malla kings, the pagodas soaring up to the overcast sky, and the masked dancers roaming the streets. Thus the divine

Myth in Space and Time in Patan

birth of Krishna tries to perform primordial time and space in the metropolis which is a reluctant city, a city loves to evoke the primordial.

The reluctance is what the nature of the city is, almost all the cities of the valley. The inclination is the myth, the folk time and space. The Newar mind of the valley creates constant cultural return to the myth as if to look for the psychological healings. Return to the myth is the return to innocence of the ritualistic performances, of deinstitutionalization of religion as a system of code. Krishna-like decorated babies with their mothers is the memory of the folk. The mythic-folk created space is the time of leisure without any sense of hurriedness and urban speed.

Why is the anatomy of a city informed by the celebration of myths? Celebration is an ontological necessity, a necessity of symbolization for survival in those spaces which are mundane and teleological and may be forgettable for some times. Why is mythical psyche so very significant to perform? Can institutionalized religions allow a goat sacrifice at the alter of Krishna who is a vegetarian in institutionalized Brahministic Hindu conceptualization which is unimaginable in common religious creeds? If the sacrifice makes the victim sacred at a divine alter, then the animal is conceived sacred in any ritual-religious space, in a Krishna or a Kali temple[1].

This is where the mythic consciousness prevails over the codes of religion. The very idea that some gods seek blood, the others are satisfied with flowers and sweets, the rituals of sacrifice cuts across the divisionism of animal-sacrifice seeking deity and peace loving supernaturals, and the canonical Hindu categorization of who is a vegetarian deity and who accepts flesh and blood. The Hindu epics have textual variations in time and space and many characters do

---

[1] See page 1 in Rene Girard. (2005). *Violence and the Sacred*. Trans. Patrick Gregory. London: Continuum.

JANMASTAMI

Krishna in Tantra shrine

not appear as they feature in canonical epics like *the Ramayana* and *the Mahabharata*. Krishna in *Srikula* tantric tradition[2] is associated with Lalita or Tripurasundari (Goudriaan and Gupta: 1981: 71). The Krishna temple in Hanumandhoka is called Chyasin Dega and Vansagopal which is in octagonal shape suggestive of tantric symbolism.

In *Tantraraja Tantra*,[3] Tripurasundari takes the form of Krishna, who belongs to Mahavidaya tradition of tantric deities of knowledge. Krishna is the consort of all the Mahavidayas according to *Todala*

---

[2] The Mahavidya deities are grouped in two kulas or families, Kalikula which includes Kali, Tara, Bhuvaneswori) and Srikula included Lalita-Tripurasundari, Bhairavi, Baglamukhi, Kamala, Dhumbawati, Matangi, and also Chamunda and Chandi who are not identified as the Mahavidya goddesses). Kalikula deities are popular in regions of Nepal, Assam and Bengal, and Srikula in Southern regions of India.

[3] See the text edited by Avalon Arthur and Lakshamana Sastri

Tantra: Bhagavati Kali is the image of Krishna,[4] which suggest both to the color and personality of the Kali as Krishna or Krishna as Kali. Such association of Krishna with power deities of tantric tradition may have the god's connection with sacrifice rituals in the valley. The idea of sacrifice is not limited to killing an animal. There are metaphoric explanations of sacrifice as the act of devouring the evil in you but such explanations are just one set of the interpretations about the idea of sacrifice as escaping from the realistic tradition of sacrificing animals. The killing of an animal at Krishna temple is the ritual of myth as the moment of double bind where killing as sacred can happen even at the very alter of Vaishnav super god, the god who enacted in multiple forms as avatars in the myths and epics of the Hindu tradition. Furthermore, the celebration is the act of joy on the birth of the god which is manifested by sacrifice of animals, and at times disavowed as inhuman.

The celebration of the myths as rituals and the necessity of symbolization for survival are two of the most significant traits of the valley culture. Celebration and symbolization are the sublime warp holes in time. They not only give meaning to life by the use of the myths as past, they speak about the aesthetics of the mind of the people who are surrounded by deities, temples, and palaces. Consequently, celebration and symbolization are the anatomy of the city as the collective psyche to perform. At times, the performances may unnerve the visitors when a selected buffalo is chased as a demon and is killed in a square. The blood is spilled in surprising sacrificial paradoxes. "Because the victim is sacred, it is criminal to kill him – but the victim is sacred only because he is to be killed," writes Henri Hubert and Marcel Mauss (qtd in Girard: *Violence* 1). Still killings cannot be defended and it should not be. There was the sacred innocence involved in sacrifices when

---

[4] see chapter 10 of *Todala Tantra*: "Bhagavati Kali is the Krishna Murti."

we feared that the deities were angered if the human were unable to avoid evil acts. The buffalo or any other victim-animal turns as the symbolized evil as gifts to the supernatural. The only possible defense in killing is the relationship with the deities in psychological terms, that she desires blood to bring peace to the world: myths function in such ironical practices. Rituals do not entail logic[5] but emotions of fear about diseases and disasters and releasing such fears are enacted in the domain of mythical narratives and rituals, beliefs in the supernatural and carrying them in traditions.

There is a tradition of 'seu' eating or eating of the parts of the goat head: eyes, tongues, ears. The parts are distributed by caste identity. Abhash Rajopadhyaya[6] told us that the local myths tell that Krishna has Shiva connection. Kali or Mahamaya too is worshipped during Janamastami. According to the local myths, Mahadev always teased Kali for being black[7] and she was unhappy about it. She then wished him to be born as a black person and he as a fair girl. Consequently, he became dark Krishna and Kali as the fair Radha. Thus Krishna shares the essence of Mahadeva and shares a bond with Kali. The same images from Krishna temple shrine is installed

---

[5] I use logic in a conventional sense of the term because myths may have its own logic which may not correspond with logic of two plus two are four, or what we understand by deductive and inductive modes of argumentation.

[6] Renuka Khatiwada and I had a long walk around Basantapur, Kathmandu Durbar Chauk with Abhash Rajopadhyaya. He was an M. Phil (English) student from Institute of Advanced Communication, Education, Research (IACER), Kathmandu. He also is a scholar on Newar Hindu and Buddhist tradition.

[7] A Bengali tantra text *Kalivilasa Tantra* narrates almost a similar story of Krishna being fair when he was born as the son of Durga and due to his passionate excitement he was turned dark. Fairness and its association with divinities is 'light skin' ideology of color which contemporary discourse rejects as racist and bias mindsets. My purpose is to refer to stories and anecdotes of all kinds without being critical at times.

in Mohankali Chauk in Falgun Purnima. The mythical association of Janamasthami with Kali, as I have mentioned before, may have paved ways for animal sacrifice in Krishna cult. Krishna Temple in Basantapur is in octagonal shape which gives it a tantric structure. Thus the celebration with animal meat is vernacular mingling of the divinity from diverse divine identities of local and canonical narratives and rituals.

We return to the celebration of the birth of Krishna. A multifaceted hero of the myths and epics, of literature and the arts. A mischievous village lad, shepherd, warrior, yogi, guru, lover, politician, friend, and the traveler across time and space. His rank as supreme deity varies in Hindu texts.

> In the Mahābhārata, Harivaṃśa and Viṣṇu Purāṇa, there is no doubt that Kṛṣṇa is an incarnation of Viṣṇu. The roles, for the most part, have been somewhat reversed in the Bhāgavata: while there are abundant passages in the text that relate to Viṣṇu without explicitly subordinating him to Kṛṣṇa, particularly in the books prior to the tenth, the general thrust of the tenth book prioritizes Kṛṣṇa. In many ways, the very structure of the Purāṇa culminates in the story of Kṛṣṇa's incarnation, with the first nine books forming a prologue to the full glory of Bhagavān in the tenth book, which, as was noted, takes up a quarter of the entire twelve books of the Purāṇa. (Kemmerer: 2003: 27-28).

The birth of the god is supernaturally mysterious. Kansa had killed six sons of his sister Devaki because the eighth son, as predicted, would be the cause of his death. Out of fear, he started killing all the babies born to her sister. Devaki got pregnant for the seventh time. Lord Vishnu had asked goddess Yogmaya to extract part of the embryo and transform it into the womb of Rohini, wife of Vasudeva of Vajra. "8. The embryo in the womb of Devakī is my own Śakti [power], known as Śeṣa. After you have extracted him, transfer him into the womb of Rohiṇī." Viṣṇu tells the goddess that the remaining part will appear as Devakī's son. "9. Then I, with my aṃśa [partial incarnation], I will appear as the son of Devakī, O auspicious one, and you will manifest in Yaśodā, the wife of Nanda." (Kemmerer: 2006:164)

> 18. In due time, queen Devakī bore the manifestation of the infallible Lord, the source of auspiciousness for the whole world, and the soul of everything, who was contained within her. He had been deposited there by Vasudeva, the son of Śūra, by mental transmission.4 Devakī looked like the [eastern] quarter which bears the pleasure-giving moon. (166)

The sign of the divine made her radiant. Krishna was to be born like his previous incarnations as Vamana, Parasurama, Rama, Hamsa, Varaha, Nrsimha, Kurma, Hayagriva, and Matsya (dwarf, a Brahmin, a chatriya, a swan, boar, man-lion, tortoise, horse and fish respectively). At the time of his birth, the constellation was Rohini, and the world was in abundance with nature and happiness.

> 9–10. Vasudeva saw that amazing, lotus-eyed child, his four arms wielding the weapons of the conch, club, lotus and disc.5 He bore the mark of śrīvatsa, and the Kaustubha jewel was radiant on his neck.6 Clad in a yellow garment, he appeared as beautiful as a dark rain-cloud. He was resplendent with a magnificent belt, and arm and wrist bracelets, and his profuse locks were encircled with a lustrous helmet and earrings made of valuable vaidūrya gems. (175)

Krishna's birth is celebrated in Nepal and India with utmost joy. The valley in particular turn into processions.

The outer waves of rainy cloud look at the pinnacles of the temples in Patan. The crowd is aware of the nature and art hovering over and witnessing. Amidst all the coming together of nature, art and human, there are humming, laughing, giggling, screaming with the sound of music. Looking upon the crowd from a distance is to understand the memory of the city which has continued with the birth of an epic character. The evening tames the present-modern[8] to the folk, and nature and art collaborating with the humans; the present-modern is nearby outside of the courtyard as cars and malls, and speeding plane reaching out to other cities. Once the collaboration is visible, the folk comes unfolding upon us in the very space of the present-modern.

---

[8] Our argument about present-modern is about how every phase is modern in its own terms. Hence, there are moderns in the past: every phase has its own moderns. Hence, the use of the term.

HARITALIKA TEEJ
The Double Bind of Happiness

The festival of fasting by women for the well being of their husbands, men of their love and also for their selves is a colorful spectacle in Nepal. The festival of Teej is dedicated to fasting and dancing and finally having a rich food on the day called *darkhane*, when women eat staple food like *khir*, *puri*, and *sweets*[1]. After the first day of *darkhane*, the second day is that of fasting, going to temples, and dancing in groups. The third day is Rishi Panchami[2] when seven divine sages are worshipped. The seven sages are Kashypa, Atri, Bharadwaj, Vishwamitra, Gautama, Jamadagni, and Vashishtha.

My discourse on Teej does not represent only the urban class women and men who probably are the significant lower percentage in Nepal and northern India. I am also aware that Teej is not merely a festival of strict fasting nowadays but celebrating and locating women's agency through such aesthetic acts. One also knows that Teej in Nepal in early times was celebrated by married women going to mother's home, an example of further locating agency

---

[1] Khir or kheer is sweet rice pudding made by boiling milk with rice and sugar. Puri is deep fried puffed bread of whole wheat flour.

[2] The term Panchami suggests the fifth day, particularly the fifth day of Shukla paksha (waxing moon period) in the Nepali month of Bhadra. It may sometimes fall on the following day of Darkhane or a day after, depending on the Hindu calendar.

Women in Ritual

through her association with the home of childhood. The following discourse is based on my engagement with women who are my students, academics, family members, and public individuals.

The paradox of happiness comes at a cost which we never can put aside during our journey in the city. A woman repeated the patriarchal construct when Renuka asked about not drinking water. Drinking water during the fast is like drinking the blood of the husband[3]. Pallabi Gupta[4] had a conversation with me. She told that a woman drinking water during the fasting is demonic for the male ideologized creed; it is the same story of women as a demon or as an angel: she has the power to kill (by drinking 'blood') and as the power to protect by not drinking water. It is an age old patriarchal stamp on what women should, critiqued Pallabi and Renuka. Not only Teej, but many of the Hindu festivals do not escape the male

---

[3] "Pani khaye pachi sriman ko ragat khaye jasto huncha," it is a Nepali saying by many traditionally devout women.

[4] Pallabi is my daughter who teaches English at University of Illinois, Urbana-Champaign. I had a long conversation with her on March 1, 2021. She further elaborated what she critiqued by email.

prescriptions though many festivals like Teej are coming out of the patriarchal codes of religious behavior, especially among the urban women, who arguably rarely represent the vast countryside of South Asia in terms with claims to empowerment and agency.

Though for a small percentage of educated urban women do not follow regressive rituals but a majority of women do, says a graduate student. The narratives are empowering. One of the major rituals in the day is performed as women clean themselves from the sin of impurities of menstruation blood. This is the most regressive patriarchal ideology, the student was adamant. There are multiple mythical stories associated with the origin of the ritual. Brahma, the creator god tells the story of a widow, daughter of Uttank and Sushila who had defiled the kitchen by entering into the space when in menses. She had committed that sin in her previous life and she is now attacked by ants all over her body. A learned patriarch comes and rescues her by asking her to consecrate her body and soul on

Sharing in the Water

the day of Rishi Panchami. Women go to the rivers and clean their teeth with *neem* twigs used as brushes. *Rishi Panchami Vrata Katha* (*The tale of Fasting in Rishi Panchami*) is a popular text full of stories of women as sinners for defiling sacred places while in menstruation cycle.

My interpretations and opinions on Teej may be that of an outsider as a male and at the same time interpretations are necessary for academic purpose. My ideas, however, are influenced by the women with whom I have academic interactions. Teej, therefore, cannot be a matter of outside scholarly debate. The implied apology is directed toward an event. Many years ago in a seminar I had presented a paper in which I had commented on the rituals involved in Teej. Many of my female and male colleagues had defended the rituals of dance and celebrating the ritual as women's choice. One of my colleagues had retorted that she was happy to celebrate the festival by keeping fast, dancing, and cleansing herself, there should not be any problem from others, she had retorted. Such ideologies are prevalent in many women and men when a ritual, however inappropriate it may be, represents age-old values. The sharp criticism which had followed by students than teachers had retorted that happiness is internalization of male ideology. The debate was tense and productive around what then is 'internalization of ideology'.

Is ideology the instrument of domination, hegemony, and oppression? How amidst systematic hegemony and/or oppression of the margin, even scopes of celebration from regressive rituals open both the doors to happiness and do not. The dominant male religiosity allows times and gives space to be happy as respites, and happiness thus becomes real, true, and honest. Happiness is not questioned or doubted but the roots of happiness may be problematic because happiness is constructed/created, scoped within patriarchal normativity. Happiness is allowed as oppression is allowed on the margin. "I do not follow Teej at all. I do not like to perform as a sinner for my biological essence."5

Yet the celebrations are real and lively, the dances and parties are unpretentious. "The festival provides liberating spaces for women despite knowing fasting is salutary," commented a doctoral student. The very space is both the space prescribed by the rituals of patriarchy and space providing joy.

The goddess who represents the devotion of the wife toward the husband is Parvati and her lord is Shiva6. Parvati is the epitome of devotion and hence is the ideal mythical figure for the festival. There are many varieties of Teej festival in South Asia, but in Nepal Haritalika Teej is celebrated.

Purification

The very circumstances of limitations imposed by the institutions of power, religion or patriarchy, for instance, allow celebration. Even hunger is celebrated as satisfaction within the circumstances of poverty; hunger thus is internalized as fate and to be happy by accepting fate. 'We are poor but we are happy' has been an ideological prescription through stories and movies, and at times by the ruling classes. The 1992 novel *The City of Joy* by Dominique

---

5 A student spoke and the two of her friends laughed recalling what the male members of her family act pious during the festival. The informal talk was after the class at IACER at the beginning of 2018 Fall semester.

6 In many of the tantra and Purana texts related with Shiva and Parvati, it is almost always Parvati asks and Shiva answers as a better person of wisdom and information. Prof. Gayatri Spivak Chakarbarty once reminded me never to forget gender bias from Plato to Durga Puja, nationalism to sports.

Lapierre is a beautiful novel of the same 'poor but happy' ideology. It represents the mindset of finding spiritualism in the slums.

Happiness within hunger or happiness within Teej is determinism, an ideology. A helper associate, a half-slave at a Jamindar house in Kapilabastu had told me something like this, a very double bind of empowerment, "I am satisfied because I eat by my hard work, my sweat, and thus I am happy." Happiness is true and honest, it is real but it comes out the space of limitation, scarcity, lack of opportunities, and oppression by the landlord to let him 'freely' work hard and earn and eat for two generations. The empowerment falls apart like the happiness in Teej may fall apart.

One constructs happiness out of patriarchal normativity to make women happy. The happiness for both men and women come out of narrative hegemony. The tales are told or the tales are referred as coming from the divine mouth of Brahma who cannot be wrong, the staunch believer claims. The great patriarch has four divine heads and whatever he pronounces are sacred laws. He not only tells the story of a girl but a widow who in her previous life had sinned by going to a cooking place during her menses. The narrative defilement of woman is characterized on two levels, that she is a widow, an unfortunate woman living with her parents after the death of the husband and thus she is suggestively discarded by her in-laws. The other is that she carries the sin with her in her next birth. The patriarchs are the sages who have the power to rescue the unfortunate women across lives; a very constructed power regime across births.

The tale of the widow is threatening to women who dare to defy the codes of behavior. The textual power is circulated in almost every traditional household; circulation not as reading the texts like *Rishi Panchami Vrata Katha* but as instructions passed on from generation to generation. Reading such texts is not reading per se but is listening to women's glories in ritual readings by the priests.

HARITALIKA TEEJ

The glorified women are *pativrata*[7], the women who have taken the vow for the husband to be at his service, the *sati* woman, the most virtuous who used to go to the funeral pyre after husband's death, and woman as scarifying mother. Reading is ideology where an elderly woman does not necessarily read the text but repeats the glorification which is repeated by the previous elder.

Reading is getting threatened, being instructed, listening, repeating. Reading is a cultural form associated with assimilation of conducts imparted by canonical scripture, tales recited by pandits, approved by men to celebrate. Reading is preoccupation with the form of ritual which is structured as celebration where men are at a distance observing or disinterested and women are busy shedding their sins with water and by the blessings of the sages residing up in the sky.

A male friend told me that his wife and daughter just listen to the tales and do not pay attention to what is recited. The problem that he cannot stop not reading such texts underlies 'the rule of the father'. If both not reading and reading are the choices, the wife and daughter empower themselves and the husband too, and also the community at large. The number of *Satyanarayan Brata Katha* texts are sold in a city like Kathmandu reveals the code behind the friend's comments.

Codes for women's behavior is the production and celebration as happiness. Teej has developed into a status symbol in such process of production and reception. The middle class urban women liberate themselves with performances by reserving hotels and restaurants which are statements of pure celebration. The very space of women is also the space of freedom where no one bothers about the tales of scriptural conduct but occupies a space with one another, says a

---

[7] Pati in Nepali (with its Sanskrit origin) means husband and Vrata mean vow. To keep Vrata means to fast.

· 45 ·

The Monuments of Sacred

corporate employee. She told me that she does not know about *Vrata* stories and knows only that it is a festival to enjoy with dancing and eating. Her friend retorted that the urban middle class celebration is not a celebrating phenomena but for millions of women in the vast spaces of Nepali and Indian countryside, it is a code of performing idealism. Such acts of urban celebration influence millions of women in the countryside as codes of idealism. A practicing Hindu, a scholar from Bangladesh whose in-laws celebrate *Karwa Chauth* by the influence of Indian soap operas told me, "Such festivals are as powerful as patriarchal codes; we should be careful about how and why we do it." A practicing Muslim faculty from Dhaka participated in the discussion and added, "Hijab may be a fashion statement for urban middle class women but it is a necessity for women in the countryside, and you see, Hijab as a fashion statement and choice of women is ambiguous dress code. One has to put it on as soon as one goes out, a regularity, a necessity in public space is ambiguously fashionable." It is a pressurized happiness, her argument is[8]. The other girl emphatically told us that she waits for the festival of *Karwa Chauth* and no one objects in her home in Chittagong. An M. Phil. student from Pokhara smiled, "My wife looks beautiful during the festivals, in red sari and glowing face." Language represent ideology. Perhaps there are no unideologized statements. "When I return home from the college, if I do not see my wife at home, I get upset," opinionated a colleague. Such statements reveal the deep sheeted code of patriarchy.

My argument about urban celebration is ambiguously premised because the choice of 'waiting' and the statement of looking beautiful are both male construct coded for women in general and at the same time, a time of the year for celebration only or suggestively during festivals only. Does celebration represent all rituals as freedom or celebration is internalized prescription? It is like the *hijab* as fashion statement by middle class urban women. But it is an imposition for millions of women in South Asia; covering the face with *ghoonghat*[9] in the heat of the Indian summer cannot be a fashion statement which otherwise is performed on ramps in many fashion fares, Renuka argues while writing a paper for a course on New Women. The *hijab* or *Ghoonghat* as fashion is a construct of patriarchal constraint. When there is no choice, the remaining option is to make the constraint as pop cultural wear, Renuka emphasizes, she told, accompanying me in a shooting day out.

The texts of Teej *katha* or Teej *Vrata Katha* is popular among Nepalis and Indians during the festival. It has multiple popular variations in websites praising the sacrifices of 'mother Parvati' to

---

[8] In December 2020, I interviewed my former students who are working individuals in private firms. I have not identified the students

[9] *Ghoonghat* is a head or face covering by the part of the sari.

get Shiva as her husband prescribing strong suggestions that this is what women should do by venerating the goddess as their ideal.

The text has been the site of oppression. Anna Yeatman talks about "different bases of oppression," she continues:

> that is, working with the idea that there are multiple bases of oppression, that is there is class, gender, ethnicity, race, sexuality, and that not any one of these bases of oppression can be viewed as a master key to the rest, that they have to be treated analytically separately and then examined in their historically specific intersections. (137: 1997)

South Asian Hindu imagination, to be particular, is textually driven. If the myths as narrative are textual, it is claimed to be historical. Since the adventures of the gods and goddesses, demons, and semi-divine beings are written elaborately, they become historical for many Hindu South Asians. Even the use of the word 'myth' is offensive to many of them I know. What is written religiously in series and volumes becomes sacred. It does not matter who wrote them. Sangari and Vaid write: "The Vedic (and later, the Puranic) model becomes both a part of popular consciousness as well as of organized reform such as that of the Arya Samaj and is fed into the companionate models of he middleclass family" (2006: 10). Thus the textual becomes historical and historical becomes models.

During my conversation[10] with Renuka, she told me about the dresses worn by Hindu women during festivals. They are uncomfortably overloaded, especially, the attire of the bride. "Wearing heavy gold bangles, jewelries, payal[11], stone-stud

---

[10] Feb. 23, 2021.

[11] *Payal* in anklet which are made mainly of silver which come in various designs

embroidered saris obstruct movements from walking, sitting to eating. The facial makeups make women uncomfortable while eating; the glasses and stones in the sari scratch skins. They are mechanisms of patriarchal dress codes which women internalize as necessary embellishments. The disciplining is determined by the woman's concern about her dress with which she has to walk, to be careful about her gait, and to be careful about not damaging the expensive dress. Hand movements are controlled with abundance of bangles. Women share that they go through the most uncomfortable times during weddings and festivals. Men have little to worry about because they put on three piece suits or formal dresses of their ethnic traditions."

She added, "Sari is the symbol of constraint which males prefer, which is the symbol of male ideological preference. By the means of sari males do not have to control women, it is quite a disciplining attire and men do not have to do much. Men unconsciously like women to wear the *savya*[12] dress. I slipped out into the ideology when once I asked my close friend to put on Sari for a documentary shoot. She put me into task. We slip into ideologies. Another friend from India never liked her daughter in-law to use the family name of the 'father's' home (the title comes in the male line of descent, almost globally).

Renuka always tells me that she feels proud when she puts on sari and do photography. "At that moment I control the camera and focus on the work instead of managing the sari. I just do not care. That is the moment of not being controlled by the male mechanism, male preference. Thus neither I have to control the dress nor the dress controls me whereas the dress is a controlling attire for men."

Our conversations during the walks are critical. "Despite sari is a dress which controls movements and is a preferred attire by

---

[12] *Savya* connotes to sophisticated mannerism.

The Dancing Woman in Teej

the male as it an idealism performed on women, I find no logic in disliking it because men like it. Why do I have to dislike which is a controlling object? Why do I have to dislike emotions because they prefer emotions as attributes of weakness for women? Why should I not shy despite it being a male attribute of women's trait of weakness by male normativity? Since men prefer women wearing traditional dresses, women do not have to hate them. Heterronormal sexual behavior is natural for many women (like lesbian sex is normal for many women), one does not have to dislike it because men like it. I do not see "voting out" slogan as a radical feminist stand. Irrespective of men liking it or not, it is my choice to wear dress or behave in my ways. I do what my agency requires. Thus the preference of the dress or body is my preference and I use them as I like to use. Many of my friends deliberately like to be submissive by wearing sari by looking for occasions. While I do not look for occasions to wear sari, I wear even when I photograph," Renuka spoke her mind.

She hit hard on the women who still drink the water washed out of the feet of husband. It is not a forbidden tradition, she informs. "Though women deny that they drink the washed water of husband's feet whom I have witnessed during such acts of drinking, while working on wedding photography. At many occasions I am not to click such images. Women do because their acts, they think, are to be obedient to their men. Many don't know why they do. Many claim that they fast for themselves not for husbands. But the paradox is that fasting happens only on the occasions of Teej and other festivals," Renuka concluded.

Thus Teej is a festival of agency for many urban women, a time to be with friends, a performance which comes once a year. The nature of Teej is changing in urban spaces from patriarchal hegemony to gender consciousness. A colorful festival both of agency and ideology makes women impose their emancipatory desires despite the patriarchal determinism.

INDRA JATRA
The Agrarian Negotiation and the Rationale of Cruelty

Narrations behind the festivals are the conditions of performances. The performances as rituals and celebration in the valley are to venerate the king of heaven, Indra. As the myth goes, the Jatra evolved out of a negotiation between the valley people and the mother of the Gods, Aditi. By bestowing the gift of fog and dew in the autumn, the heavenly mother negotiated the release of her

The Hands of the Procreator

son from the imprisonment. Indra was imprisoned by the locals in a valley village while stealing mimosa flower which his mother needed for worship.

The agrarian motive behind the festival of Indra - as the god was released with fun and fare - is the consequence of goddess descending to earth. Gayatri Spivak writes, " ... the Sanskrit word for "incarnation" (*avatar*) – has nothing to do with "putting on flesh." It means rather – "a come-down being [being]." Everything around is, after all, "come down," if we assume an "up there." (2012: 182). She is forced to descend to the earth to rescue her son, the supernatural energy is invested in to appear from the sky above to free the thief. The tree is earthly and the garden of heaven lacks the flower. There are two parallel metaphors of supernatural fact, one of the lack and the other of the descent. They both are linked because Indra descends to take the exclusive flower and the mother descends to bestow gift. The act of stealing leads to the act of negotiation which results in celebration and performances, as the agrarian art of the valley.

The acts of the mother, Indra, and the farmers are agrarian in essence, and art as celebration comes as a mode of fulfilment of the essence. The myth encompasses the supernatural, natural, and the art. The wish of the mother finally results in the ripening of the season by the moisture of the mother's milk around the abundance of whiteness: the white mimosa, fog, and dew.

Aditi is the primordial mother, mother of all gods. She also has promised to take the souls of the dead along with her. Mother thus is the redeemer in multiple forms who ultimately takes a backstage in the entire Indra Jatra festival. Why is the deity forgotten in the season of joy? We do not know why. The imprisonment of the supernatural thief takes the central stage as the victory of the people. The god is paraded every year.

Indra Jatra is a week long festival of unprecedented spectacle, which displays Yosin Thanegu when yosin or linga is erected with

Hoisting Ya Sin, the Phallus

wooden poles. Kumari Jatra is celebrated by pulling chariots in the different parts of the old cities. *Dagin* (*Aditi*) is busy in search for her son. Additionally *Pulu Kisi* is the dance of the elephant when Indra had arrived to look for the flower, and Majipa Lakhey, the benign Bhairava[1] performs *Sawo Bakhu*, the demon dance. Thus capturing of the god is reflected in the spectacle of celebration in forms of demon dance and visiting the shrines; even Shiva dances as participant in the spectacle. There also is the procession of Kumari, the virgin goddess, and animal sacrifices in some parts of the city.

    The aspect of cruelty is the most significant imagery of the festival. Cruelty has always been the feature of mythical recurrence in art, literature, and rituals. There is no justification of immense cruelty on animals to justify the annihilation of the evil which animals are attributed to or symbolized as. Mythical mimesis in

---

[1] Bhairava is a form of Hindu god Shiva.

ritualism makes the weakest, the scapegoats. In the ancient cultures from ancient Phoenicia where humans were the scapegoats to modern urban space like the Kathmandu valley where buffaloes are the representation of demon evil, there are continued performances of using the weak as the evil.

Why do we consider the weak as the demon is such rituals? Is the weak social unwanted, a bizarre political act of annihilation of the fragile. Weak in this sense is not physical fragility but defenselessness of the animals. Religious criminality is the justification of self onto the other. Religion at large has functioned on the other as unwanted, as devil, non-religious, heathen, *kaffir*, *maleksha*[2]. The annihilation is the survival mask of the strong, a mode of justice done by killing the other.

In a more metaphoric way, the blood takes the form of a flower, or the flower is the blood on the alter of the deity. The two very diverse objects of nature first come together as metonymy, both combined in a horizontal relationship, and then turns metaphor, one replaces the other: flower is *prasad*[3] like the blood is *prasad*. Mythical mind performs such a cruelty from the ancient times to the present. The *prasad* is not for survival of the innocent primal tribal imagination but a pure cruelty in the recent times, devoid of ancient innocence. But the myth is ritual which is and has to be followed.

Scapegoating is a negation of the self with the constructed demon. The demon is always out there, not within me, but outside me. I have to annihilate the other by concretizing the demon as animal. The animal suits my purpose because something not human is easily demonic. The cruel is constantly overpowering aspect of the

---

[2] *Kaffir* is an Arabian term for infidel. The Sanskrit term *Maleksha* suggests to non-Aryans.

[3] *Prasad* is the offering to the god which the devotees share.

human psyche hence the animal as the symbolic of cruelty is both becomes the victim and gift from the gods to humans as *prasad*.

The irony is that Indra Jatra cannot function without the blood because the victory of the human over divinity makes human wild in celebration. A puzzling question for Rene Gerard is, "Why, for example, do we never explore the relationship between sacrifice and violence?" (2005: 2). Violence is generally justified by the one who commits to violence: state justified the enemy state, killing is justified as taking fitting revenge on the victim but sacrificial violence is displacement of the object-evil as sacrificial object. "… all victims, even the animal ones bear a certain resemblance to the object they replace; otherwise the violent impulse would remain unsatisfied" (12). Girard further states, "the proper functioning of the sacrificial process requires not only the complete separation of the sacrificed victim from those beings for whom the victim is a substitute but also a similarity between both parties" (41). Displacement works both as separation and similarity, the separation with the person or community is about the other, the animal as the evil, and the similarity is the object killed become *prasad*, pious as the devotee is by performing the act of serving the food to be the *prasad*. Displacement further works as an object to be killed to be displaced as acceptable and agreeable. Gerard explains:

> To understand how and why sacrifice functions as it does, we should consider the proposition that the ritual victim is never substituted for some particular member of the community or even for the community as a whole: *it is always substituted for the surrogate victim*. As this victim serves as substitute for all the members of a community, the sacrificial substitution does indeed play the role of that we have attributed to it, protecting all the members of the community from their respective violence – but always through the intermediary of the surrogate victim. (106-107)

The animal is thus distanced and at the same time close to the community, sacred even before the killing.

Sacrifice is the essential part of almost all the festivals of the Hindus. The dance is another, and seen in a varieties of modes. *Pulu Kisi* is the dance of elephant for his master Indra, *Majipa Lakhey* is the dance of benevolent *Bhairava*, and the *Sawo Bhaku* demon is the dance after slaughtering a buffalo.

The dancers use masks of the deities and demons to demonstrate the other which they become. More than the disguise, it the the manner of becoming the other. It is the representation of the supernatural. Masks assimilate the other to be able to find the very mask which the unmasked self is; mask is within the performing individual, the multiple shades of self within, instead of conceiving it that "primitive people" were 'obsessed with "disguises",' writes Girard (2005: 176). The human is the site of all that he or she

The Mask Dancers

An artist's final touch on Sweta Bhairava.

performs. He does not have to disguise. Mask unfolds the multiple selves. The mask is he.

One of the last rites of the Jatra is *Hathwo-hayekegu* ritual, the wine flowing outside from the mouth of Bhairava as *prasad* which the devotees in the evening drink with a loud fanfare. The shouting and rapturous women on their day become a liberating site for the viewers. The smell of the ale takes the world in a remoteness of rapturous raw nature. It is a further negotiation with the multiple selves which she has assimilated as an evolving human being. The negotiation of the inner and outer, evil and good, wild and sober, and many such human doubles as well as overlapping characteristics.

Indra Jatra is not only dear to the valley people but is the essence of their faith which motivates to perform myth as necessity for human behavior. The myth is the symbol of beliefs and attitudes which is realized as stories, wisdom, rituals, legends, histories, and supernatural. Such multiple realizations of myth cannot be fictional because it lives with in multiple forms.

MAHADASHAMI
The Mystic Smile in the Act of Killing

The Sacred Drummer

Durga, the most revered of the deities, brings forth a long awaited festival, which becomes the occassion of week to month long vacations in the country. Like many of the Indian communities, Nepal too gives elaborate ritualistic significance to the deity. She is popular by many names in the valley though these names at times have local origins instead of being merely Vedic in canonical sense.

Uma, Parvati, Kali, Bhawani, Bhairavi, and Taleju are some of the popular names but she also known as *mais* or mothers and devis as Pathivara Mai, Paltamai, Jakhadi Mai, Kankai mai, Vatsala Devi, and hundreds of local Durgas in Nepal. She is also associated with group of goddesses like the Mahavidyas, Navadurgas, and Matrikas, the goddesses of knowledge, nine-Durgas, and mother goddesses respectively. The local deities are not the forms of Durga because they may have evolved as independent deities. The association of the goddesses with Durga is casually popular connectivity.

The origin of Durga has Indus valley roots. Mohenjo-Daro seal M-1186 depicts a priest with a human head in front of him. There are seven women at the bottom who probably are the seven mothers. The seal is supposed to be first of the images depicting goddess figures along with the series of terracotta mother goddesses. Describing M-1186, Asko Parpola suggests, "The tree is probably the banyan fig, and the deity inside it a predecessor of Durga, the goddess of victory and love, to whom a human sacrifice of a brave warrior has been made" (qtd. in Samuel 2009: 4). The reference to the deity comes later in the Vedic tradition too. "Devisukta" in the *Rg Veda* contains the proclamations of the goddess. *Devi Bhagwat Purana*[1] is also about the acts and glories of the goddess. Sage Vyas who is the author of the *Mahabharata* is also credited with the composition of the 18 Puranas. Vyas's disciple Sutaji talks about *Devi Bhagawat Purana* to the sages and his students. He tells them that his guru Vyas had recited and explained the text to Janmejaya, the descendent of the Pandus.

In Nepal, the festival begins in pre-winter, September or October, in the bright lunar phase with *Ghatasthapana*, which

---

[1] See "Introduction" *Devi Bhagwat Puran*. Ed. Dr. Vinay. Dimond Books, edition: 2016, Delhi). See the most popular text on the glory of the goddess "Devimahatyam" of *Markandeya Purana*.

MAHADASHAMI

is placing a pot or *kalasha* with holy water within, along with *jamara* [2] and flowers. The ritual of *Phulpati* occurs on the seventh day of Dashain or Dashera, the popular Nepali and North India references to Durga Puja festival respectively. *Phulpati* is an official religious ritual which is performed in the central park, Tundikhel, in Kathmandu. *Maha Asthami*, is day of appearance of Kali who emanated by Durga to kill the demons, *Maha Navami*, the ninth day of the ceremony, and *Vijaya Dashmi*, the day of victory are the most significant phases of the festival. Finally, with *Kojagrat Purnima*, on the full moon day, the Goddess Lakshmi descends on the earth to bless the devotes. Animals sacrifice of buffaloes and goats are the major events of the festival in many communities of Nepal but there are many other communities who do not practice animal sacrifice.

The festival of goddess Durga is the assimilation of the evil into godhood. The very act of killing is metaphoric of the act of subduing the evil incarnate. The conventional imagery of the Durga in sculpture displays a mystic smile and a distant meditative look away from the target who is to be pierced by a lance while the lion, the divine carrier of the goddess pounces upon the demon Mahisasura to end the great conflict between the good and the bad. The mystic smile recalls the desire of the goddess to incorporate the evil into herself, a significant act of blessing by 'killing'. Killing thus is the act of absorption of the demon. Killing is a sublime act of merger of the evil as the medieval stone images depict.

The mythical narratives and visuals do not create an opposition between good and the bad. The classical conventional Durga and demon visuals in the very moment of clash do not project the goddess with fierce hatred toward the 'enemy'. There are key images found in Kathmandu valley where Durga's face emits the smile of

---

[2] *Jamara* is a kind of grass from barley seeds.

The Union of Divine and Demon

uniting the demon[3]. If the constant reconciliation between god and demon, good and evil is evident in Durga imagery, similar reconciliation of the opposites is manifest in other acts and events of Hindu narratives and performances.

Since Durga is the warrior, she is aggressive too. *Devimahatmya* describes the final moment of war: she jumped over the demon incarnate, kicked him with her foot and pierced her spear into his neck. In the very moment of assault, she looks at a distance, not targeting the target but emits a mystic smile. The calm smile is both the moment of her heroic deed accomplished and the return of the moment when the demons wanted to marry her but the union for her was of a dimension of divine sanctuary to the devil after the fierce war of the world.

---

[3] See Zimmer in the Works Cited. 196)

The tradition of yoga, on the one hand, and tantra, on the other, are two different traditions of the human body and mind to be disciplined. Yoga has Vedic influence and tantra has both Vedic and non-Vedic ritualistic tradition. Both are two significant traditions which take concepts like spirituality,

The sacrificed

devotion, and liberation differently and the very merger of the opposite get manifested in the arts of South Asia, for instance, as the grotesque Kali is venerated as a beautiful protecting mother. Crane faced goddess or a goddess with severed head are realized as deities of wisdom. Intense sexual union becomes holy bodily expression, sexual imagery becomes ornamentation of the walls of temples, and goddess as Salavanjika erotically evokes nature to procreate. The merger of the opposites can be realized when the Nataraja (dancing Shiva) dances surrounded within the flame of knowledge with the god himself and the demon of ignorance under his feet, Shiva performs his evening dance in cremation ground of inbetweenness which is neither this world nor the world beyond. Krishna takes Arjuna in the midst of two opposite armies, a liminality, before the war, and imparts unprecedented wisdom. So does Durga: she smiles and looks at a distance while merging the evil into godhood. The binary of good and bad, god and evil, this world or that world, knowledge and demon are reconciled in myths and arts. The most unholy is holy, the grotesque is beautiful.

Durga in Kathmandu valley has Vajrayana Buddhist connectivities. "The Devi Purana mentions Tantras and Agmas frequently and also the Pasanda (i. e. Tantrika) Buddhas who worship the divine mother in their own ways" (Radhakamal

Sending away the Goddess, Bhaktapur

Mukherjee: 1984: 268). Kali is the emanation of Durga in *Devimahatamya* narrative and her resemblances are pervasive in Vajrayana Buddhist cult of the valley. Taleju, Ekajata, Vajrayogini, Khadagyogini, Pragyaparimita, Vidhyadhari, Vajragandhari, Hariti, Chhwaskamuni (Lha Mo) are the forms of mother goddesses sometimes fearful and dangerous and at times benevolent and calm. These deities may be both the local evolution or influences of the Indus Valley tradition of mother goddesses. They may have independent evolutions of folk imagination or Vedic and Mahayana Buddhist conceptualizations. Nepali Vajrayana tradition has many such deities who resemble Durga and Kali or even vice versa. The evolution of goddesses does not have singular sources because female deities have been around traditions from the Neolithic times. Earth goddess cultures have given way to Durga and Kali myths so it is natural to conceive female deities other than Indus Valley and Vedic sources. The agrarian cultural norms of supernaturalizing energies of nature as deities is evident in Durga myths also.

MAHADASHAMI

Dashain or Dashara is the return of the daughter to home. The arrival of the goddess and then her departure marks the beginning of winter sadness. The daughter is back to her husband's abode. She leaves and the nature turns barren. The very metaphor of leaving mother's abode is evident when devotees go through emotional outburst of crying and returning by sending the daughter by merging her to the river, a journey to send her to her husband[4].

Winter begins after the last rituals only punctuated by the celebration of goddess Laxmi and Kali. Winter comes with mist and fog and the festival times end till the month of February. The end of the season begins with the daughter returns to her husband: winter begins like when the Greek goddess Persephone leaves her mother Demeter for the underworld. Such deities represent the changes in seasonal cycles.

I write in my book *Goddesses of Kathmandu Valley: Grace, Rage, Knowledge*; I paraphrase some of the ideas. Goddess Taleju[5] is one of the most mysterious mythical deities in the valley. She signifies blood and water. During Mahadashami, the worship becomes sacred if the animal blood sours high up. At Mila Punchi festival in December, the holy water in a vessel or Kalasha is carried to Taleju from Changunarayan temple, the valley form of Vishnu-Narayan. (Gupto: 2018: 103-4)

The goddess is the symbol of blood and water: the blood thirsty divine who annihilates the fearful demons, she also is the one who decapitates herself to feed the starving devotees as goddess Chinnamasta. Furthermore, she is the erotic excellence as a consort

---

[4] The act of submersion of the goddess image into a river or lake is more popular in South Nepal and India. In Kathmandu, Newar community does not follow the tradition of submerging the images of Durga. They generally worship in the temples.

[5] She is named as Tulaja Bhawani too.

The Earth Goddess

of Shiva, and also the divine mother. Taleju thus is manyness. (103-4)

Goddess Taleju as a form of Devi is the patron deity of the valley. The pagoda complex in the old Palace Square in Basantapur is a three-roofed structure on five concentric plinths. Durga in her aspect as Taleju is one of the most revered deities in the valley. Goddess Tulaja Bhawani is worshipped particularly in Navami or the ninth day[6] of the Dashain festival, the night of the worship is called Kalratri, who is the seventh forms of goddess Durga in terms with her fearful form.

---

[6] The tenth day marks the culmination of the festival hence the name of the festival as Dashami, meaning tenth in Sanskrit language. In the full moon day of Kojagrat Purnima, the festival ends ritually.

TIHAR

Animal and the Self Amidst the Festival of the Lights

There are two significant selves during festival called Tihar, a common term used for the worship of the goddess Laxmi. The worship of the animals corresponds with many festivals where animals and birds are killed. But the worship of the animals has transcendental significance too, which I will discuss later. Furthermore, the festival represents the relationship between humans and animals in a paradoxical way if the entirety of religious

The Festival of Light with Buddha

festivals is taken into consideration. Both love and marginalization of animals is ambivalent in Hindu traditions. In the midst of such relationship, the worship of the self is another dimension of culture which connects worship as family and community ritualism and out of self ritualism, the self, the individual is given significance.

Laxmi Puja is the worship of goddess Laxmi. Shri or Laxmi appears in the *Rg Vedic* hymns as "Shree Sukta." The festival of lights coincides with Kali Puja in Assam, Bengal, and Bangladesh. In the Terai and north India, Dewali, Deepavali, or Laxmi Puja begins with *Dhanteras*.

Commonly called Tihar among the hilly Nepalis, the festival is one of the major religious events in Kathmandu valley and Nepal. The first day of the festival is the worship of the crow. It is called *Kag Tihar* or *Khicha Puja* for the Newars of the valley. *Kukur Tihar*, dog worship falls on the second day of Laxmi Puja. On the third day devotees worship the cow. The fourth day of the festival is *Mha Puja*, the worship of the self during Newari Swanti festival or Laxmi Puja. The fifth day of the festival is *Bhaitika*, an emotional occasion dedicated to the well being of brothers by sisters.

Crow is worshipped as the messenger of Yama, the god of death, and dog is revered as the gatekeeper of Yama. Ironically, in association with the animals, the timeless self evolves which gives solace to the demise of corporiality for the final purpose of otherworldliness as the essence of life. The transcendence is valued as the material suffering ends. Crow and dog worship is the very state of surrendering to the journey beyond where the divine heaven and fearful hell stands before the soul. Death has ritualistic

Worshipping for Salvation

significance to perform veneration to the truth of life by the humble natural objects like crow and dog. They are the symbols associated with death.

There are multiple possibilities of human association with death. Death is the acceptance of something which is authentic than the material existence. Death is not nothingness and indifference in some philosophical views. It also is not the avoidance and disgust for the morbid reality of life but death is a change from the mundane world to the possibility of the unknown, and the end of suffering. What do crow and dog do in such a comprehension of death that death releases from the worldly imbroglio?

The ordinary bird and animal, the most visible wanderer in the streets and skies become the symbols of transcendental journey. They journey beyond, to the gate of heaven and hell by the stroke of the realization of death in the festival of wealth and grace that the goddess bestows, is puzzling. Why does the festival of light and wealth coincide with the messengers of death? Such animals are not the favorite creatures in many Brahmanistic scriptures. There are various attitudes toward animals in Hindu narratives and philosophical texts. *Chandogaya Upanishad* mentions that those who act evil are born as dogs and pigs. Evil doers are born as gadflies, mosquitoes and many such insects and are unable to enjoy ritual and enjoyment and caught in the cycle of birth and rebirth (5.10). But the same dog of Yudhisthira is the dog of *Dharma*. God himself is the dog disguised as companion of the Pandavas, in the end of *the Mahabharata*. The five brothers with their common wife Draupadi make a physical journey to the heaven with the dog. They are confronted at the gate because Yudhisthira, the elder brother wants to inter into heaven with the dog who has accompanied them from the earth. The guard does not allow an animal into the heavenly abode but the prince persists and then Yama, the god of dharma transforms himself from the animal to divine. The dog is god himself.

The capacity to take the human soul to the realm of judgment is cow, dog and crow are associated with death. Except the cow, other two creatures are not venerated in religious symbolism.

Both crows and dogs are scavengers, both are cleaners and hence, ironically, impure. Keeping dogs as pets and taking care of them as family members are also favorite modern culture. Yet, the term 'dog' is used abusively. Crow is also not referred in any positive sense. They are degraded creatures in social hierarchy. Yet the worship of the beasts is important for the journey into the transcendental space. Unlike the cow, they are not the creatures of deliverance and hope. Cow delivers and hence is holy, dogs and crows pick the soul and take them to the gates of the heaven or the hell. A devout Hindu gifts a cow for the final heavenly abode. Dogs and crows are not the objects of gift and they are not sacred as the cow is.

Cow is goddess herself. The heavenly cow Kamadhenu is both the mother earth and goddess Laxmi, who blesses with prosperity and happiness. Along with the cow, snakes, rats, monkeys, elephants, and the mythical bird Gadura, all have divine associations. Many such animals are ambivalently treated in Hindu tradition. If cow becomes the object of veneration, other animals are not revered except during the festivals.

Ethically, humans-animal relation is preserved and respected in religious scriptures. But when buffalo is the symbol of demon, blood is sacred for the human while the animal goes through unbearable, excruciating pain. Barbara Noske writes:

> Ritual slaughtering, even though accompanied by a feeling of respect for the buffalo about to be slaughtered, nevertheless is a cruel business—the blood must flow. To cut the throat is a necessity; the buffalo should die slowly so that all the blood can leave the body. The animal is stabbed with spears in non-lethal places so as to make the process last. In order to

prevent the buffalo from tearing itself loose in fear, its tendons are sometimes cut before slaughtering takes place. (qtd in Kemmerer (2006: 284)[1]

How do we justify such forms of sacredness? Or is it just a religious version of pray and predator relationship where the survival of the one depends on the death of the other? Rational because animals are engage in the survivalist pray and predator relationship and humans are rational beings who act as killers, accomplished killers. Prey animals do not have choice; humans have.

The ritual killing has devotional innocence too, the human desire to please the supernatural for several mundane and spiritual purposes. The ritual killing bears the legacy of sacrifice as crisis in the present times as sacred spaces look like slaughter houses. The animal both as the evil or the offering reaches at the feet of the deity. The idea of deity is symbolic to psychological make up humans take: god or goddess as the seekers of scapegoating-psychosis of human creativity turns evil as the act of killing for the divine grace. The act of killing turns dark. I do not take 'dark' only in aversion but in the fullness of its ambiguity.

The dark is not the color black but the space of invisibility where one can act freely. Does killing take that space of invisibility? Thus the dark is a precarious space which is invisible for the viewer but the actor within it sees all. He kills. He represents all in the story of deliverance. The man who sacrifices sees that his community is delivered by the gift to the gods.

Dark is not black as the color black is associated with Lord Krishna, the Hindu mythical god, one of the incarnations of Vishnu; he is black. *Krishna paksha* is dark night period from the

---

[1] For original source, see Noske, Barbara. "Speciesism, Anthropocentrism, and Non-Western Cultures." *Anthrozoos* 10.4 (1997): 183–90.

full moon to the new moon. It is the time of the waning moon. In Sanskrit, the fortnight phase is called *Amawashya*, the phase of no moon. (*Shukla Paksha* is the phases of the bright moon). The arrival of Laxmi is welcomed by illumination from the houses to the streets. It is the festival of lights to repel darkness, not blackness.

Like the festival of lights which is the festival of family and community, the final phase of the festival is the worship of the self. The ritual is called *Mha puja*. It falls on the fourth day of Laxmi Puja which is also the beginning of Newar New Year or Nepal *Sambat*. The understanding of the self has a long discursive tradition in South Asian religion and philosophy. Who is this individual and why he or she stands so significant in the tradition which centers the god and otherworldliness as the final object of transcendental desire? The word self has long variants which are not the synonyms but are closely connected ideas. The word self is associated with soul (atman), and divinely with Brahma as the material and spiritual markers of the individual. The self is not synonymous with soul but self seeks to reach to the abstract purity called soul. We can bring some Buddhist and Hindu concetps associated with self and soul. The very idea of atman and its conception with individual soul is not accepted by Buddha.

> The Buddha denied the Brahmanical notion of *ātman* as an individual soul (*jīvatman*) that is related to the single controlling power that is Brahman, the universal soul (*parmātman*), by claiming that the view of a self (and of what belongs to a self – for that matter) is a false view (*mithyārṣṭi*). It is to the śramaṇas and Brāhmaṇas who are possessed by craving (*tṛiṣṇā*) that such a false view belongs. According to the Buddhist perspective, the 'self' (*ātman*) is the composite of the five aggregates that, due to the karmic law of dependent origination (*pratītyasamutpāda*), are selfless. Hence, also the composite is empty. The Buddha used terms such as 'self' (*ātman*) or 'inward' (*ādhyatmikā*) only

as conventional ways of expression, serving to cure worldlings (*pṛthagjana*) of the disease of false views. These aspects are discussed by Lalji 'Shravak' in *Buddha's Rejection of the Brahmanical Notion of Ātman*. (Dessein 1999: 5)

At the same time in Brahmanical Hindu philosophy, especially in the *Upnishads*. Lalji 'Shravak' writes in reference to upnishadic conceptualization:

> Individual soul has been treated as the micro of the universal soul. In course of time, both the concepts became identical. From the objective side, the ultimate reality was manifested as Brahman and this was also called ātman from the subjective side. Radhakrishnan (1958: 151) has explained the progressive development of the concept of ātman (self) through four stages: (i) the bodily self, (ii) the empirical self, (iii) the transcendental self, and (iv) the absolute self. (1999: 9)

In *Bṛahadaranyakipanishad* (=*Bṛh.*, 1-4.1) *ātman* is presumed as the primordial reality. *Ātman* is eternal in *Kaṭhopaniṣad*. Likewise, in *Muṇḍakopaniṣad*, atman is "omniscient and all wise" (9-10).

Seemingly, Newar conception is influenced by the very assertion of the self in transcendental significance and consequently the self is venerated not rejected despite the fact that Newar culture is equally influenced by Buddhist philosophical renderings. Self is taken as the location of self-awareness in the empirical realm and the worship is the confidence of the "I" in the ritualistic practices.

As the myth goes, Sukhwal got the gold from soldiers of Anand Malla, king of Bhaktapur. The soldiers were instructed by the king to collect sands on a particular time from Lakh Tirtha stream. The sand was supposed to turn into gold. As a host at Sukhwal's home the soldiers were tricked to leave the sand. Sukhwal worshiped his self with fanfare and then he proposed the king of Kathmandu Jaya

Deva Malla to pay all the debts of the state if the king commences a new calendar for the Newars. This is how the veneration of the self and new calendar year begins according to some narratives.

The celebration is associated with the mandala. The father makes two mandalas for every member of the family and one each for Yamaraj, the god of Death. Along with the father, the family participate in a ceremony of worshiping the god of death. The self, the mandala, and death are the three images which have symbolic value in *Mha* ritual. According to Milan Ratna Shakya, the mandala in particular supports the relation with ethnic psyche, more than '*vijñāna*' as mental process for '*citta*' in sacred ethno-cultural basis. In which, cognizance rules on things that occurs (SIC) in attraction and dissolving of dislike like a dream in virtual mind's thought. This outcrop of mind's thought is proven by philosophical vision (*darśana*) sensible to ritual practice (*sādhanā*). (2017: 1-2)

Shakya associates the Mandala with the mental imagery which is dream like pervasiveness, a consciousness, he tells me[2], which can encompass anger to compassion, literally encompassing everything from the concept of time to the rainbow. We should be happily engaged in the Mandala; Mandala is not out there, it is the image of all activity, it has to be envisioned. It is not just a diagram but ranges from cosmic to microcosmic level. The self too ranges in such pervasive levels, Prof Shakya told me. The self is the Mandala, he suggested, it is the cosmic body in a micro level in the vastness of the universe. We are the human being in the cosmic body. Buddhahood is the envisioning the mandala in totality.

He associates the mandala with the self while writing about *Mha* puja.

---

[2] I had a telephone talk with Prof. Milan Ratna Shakya on Aug 23, 2020

> Mandala is stylish for Buddhist origin in Newār cultural belief of the Kathmandu valley. One is vaguely aware to its inner light that shines like a spot-light of moonless-night in each being. This is the reality for praising of new year by promising hope for the goodness to next by body-worship, '*Mha-pujā*' to esteem with Mandala in practice. It meant one section of Newār. (3)

About the origin of the word, he further writes,

> Observing '*Brahma-pujā*' for cosmic dedication, which is understood by people of *Nepāh* in medieval time for the body worship, with admission of *Yogic cakra-pujā*, namely prevailing in ritual as *Cākah-pujā*, after the admission of *Gheraṇḍa Samhitā* in *Hatha-yogin* practice of *Gorakhanātha*'s followers. It was met with the philosophical admission of *Minapād* and *Matsyendranāth* in Buddhism. Thenceforth the term of '*Brahma-pujā*' is set in habit as *Mha-pujā*, in perversion of the word Brahama to Mha. (3)

Thus the idea of Brahma as the universal soul is contained in *Mha*, the individual. The idea of self is a significant philosophical concept. Nature and Spirit are fundamental notables which composes the universe according to *Vaisheshikha* school of Hindu philosophy. Nature is described in terms with Matter, Time, and Space which are independent entities and are all pervasive. The substances of Spirit are Atman (Self) and Manas (thought or mind). From Atman, Self knowledge springs and it creates qualities like love, hate, pleasure, pain, volition which are perceivable through manas (mind or sometimes understood as the internal organs). Apart from the six qualities, the other ones are Dharma (virtue, duty, moral and religious truth) and <u>Adharma</u> (unrighteousness and moral demerit) but they are not felt like the six qualities but are inferred.

Finally, <u>Bhavana</u> is the residual impression which is the mental apprehension which when contemplated becomes knowledge. The implication is that in such a philosophical understanding of canonical Hindu tradition, the vernacular knowledge about the category of the individual may have contributed or the Hindu tradition may have influence the vernacular. The idea is not the debate about who contributed whom, but the very significance given to the "I" as an all encompassing plural category, not as I in a singular individualistic sense. Thus the ideas of the self, the atman, manas have both religious and philosophical roots represented through rituals or such rituals have influenced philosophic-religious concepts. They correspond one another.

One of the key notions of preparedness of the soul for further journey has been one of the most significant ideas which have influenced South Asian Hindu imagination through religious scriptures, ritual narratives and *katha* (narrative) traditions. 'Atman is immortal' is a common class understanding. The idea is almost household commonality in Hindu homes, if not in every class. The philosophical comprehension of the transmigration of soul is not the issue but what is interesting is the narratives such as these from the *Puranas* and the *Upnishads*, or the epics which makes us understand the eternal characteristic of soul, the very foundation of the self. Here is an allegory:

> Now as a caterpillar, when it has come to the end of a blade of grass, I taking the next step draws itself together towards, just so this soul is taking the next step strikes down this body, dispels its ignorance, and draws itself together [for making the transition]. (Brh. 4.4.3 trans Hume: 1998)

The ritualistic significance is drawn from such wisdom because the believer hears such stories of ignorance and knowledge in almost every religious books to sermons.

But the Buddhist idea of the self is associated with suffering: when one is free from suffering, the self is complete, as he says, only "when no suffering comes to one."

From whatever one reins in the mind,
From that no suffering comes to one.
Should one rein in the mind from everything,
One is freed from all suffering." (p 101)[3]
3. 24 (4) 59. "Reining in the Mind" in *Samyutta Nikaya*

The self and its ritualistic practices have ancient roots in Brahamanistic Hinduism, multicultural Hindu traditions, and Buddhism. The ritual is both family and community affair. Newars of the valley perform *Mha puja* in open community spaces[4].

Except the worship of the deity for wealth and prosperity, Laxmi Puja has many associations with death and realization of the worldliness. In this very festival and glory, death is always the revered reality. The river bank as ghat is a favorite space of visitation by many devotees of the valley. Death is associated with *Ghat* or the burning yard on the banks of rivers. Such *ghats*, particularly on the premises of Shiva or Shakti temples in Kathmandu is sacred and melancholically retrospective. *Ghat* as the liminal space of two worlds has always been an emotionally speculative site in Hindu traditions of the valley.

Goddess Laxmi, on the other hand, represents all that is happiness perhaps only during such a season of the divine bring people to feel the fullness of life with lights and decoration, with exchange of gifts.

---

[3] See 3. 24 (4) 59. "Reining in the Mind" in Samyutta Nikaya.

[4] The latest ritual which we participated was at Arun Shrestha's house, a humble and very endearing time. Along with Arun's mother, his wife.

CHAATH
The Sun Worship

The Objects for the Sun

One of the most personified deities in many myths and religions of the world is the Sun. Babylonian Shamash, Egyptian Ra, native Americans narratives on the sun, sun in Brazilian Manicacas, Peru, Mexico, Maoris, Tongas of Pacific island, Dayaks of Borneo, and

I Change my Color

Japanese sun goddess Amaterasu, and the Norse sun god Sol:[1] there are sun gods and goddesses in almost every culture.

Chhath festival in Nepal and Bihar (India) is about the worship of the sun god, Surya. Chhath is one of the most celebrated festivals in the Mithila region of Nepal. It is also known as *Dala Chhath* and *Surya Shashti*[2]. In Kathmandu, ending the festive season, Chhath falls in either October or November, particularly in the Hindu month of Kartik. The festival in the month of Chaitra (March-April) is less popular. Kartik chhath is a four-day festival, the first two days are preparations, *Nahay-Khaye* and *Lohanda-Kharna*

---

[1] For detail information see William Tylor Olcott. (1914) *Sun Lore of all Ages: A Collection of Myths and Legends Concerning the Sun and Its Worship.* New York, G. P. Putnam's Sons. Ernest Busenbark. (1997). Symbols, Sex and Stars in Popular Beliefs: An Outline of the Origins of Moon and Sun Worship, Astrology, Sex Symbolism, Mystic Meaning of Numbers, the Cabala, and l\1any Popular Customs, Myths, Superstitions and Religious Beliefs. San Diego: The Book Tree.

[2] Gita Shah's M. Phil. dissertation on *Women's Role in Aesthetics and Ethics: A Study of Mithila Festivals.*

respectively. On the third day, women go to the ponds and rivers to see off the setting sun, and on the third day, the rising of the god brings joy to the worshippers. *Chhathi-maiya*, the sister of the sun, is also worshipped during the festival.

Furthermore, the *argha* is veneration to the setting sun reflected on a river, pond, or lake. The chief worshipper is called *Parvartin*. The evening-offering (*Sandhya Argh*) and the morning-offering (*Usha Arga*) are the visible aspects of the worship of the god. The Sun and the Moon and the stars who are considered as gods and goddesses are the divinities who can be seen. There are multiple celestial bodies who are seen but these two are almost immanent.

Chaath worship is primarily of the Terai and North Indian origin. Along with the people of the Terai region, Chaath is a popular festival in Uttar Pradesh, Bihar, and Jharkhanda states of India. The Kathmandu valley has symbolic ritual practices with the sun though there has not been any major festival dedicated to the Sun god.

During one of my conversations with Abhas Rajopadhyaya[3], he writes to me about the sun worship in the valley which is not directly related with the Sun but has symbolic connection with the deity. Agnishala temple has a well or a kunda dedicated to the Sun where fire burns perpetually. There is a painting outside. In almost every ritual, the sun is invoked as witness to the rituals. He writes,

> Some Narayan temples in the valley (as Changu Narayan of Bhaktapur, Til Madhav Narayan at Bhaktapur, Atko Narayan at Kathmandu, Swatha Narayan at Patan) and even the Matsyendranath are revered as the Sun-God. All these deities are also called Birinchi Narayan referring to the Sun-God. Matsyendranath's annual ritual of residing North-South

---

[3] August 6, 2021.

(i.e. Ta-Bahal in Patan and Bungamati) almost coincides with the north-south movement of the sun called Uttarayan-Dakshinayan in astrology. Sun is regarded also among the Panchayan deities of Lord Shiva (others being Vishnu, Shiva, Mrityunjaya and Aghor) and worshipped in all Shaivite rituals. So almost all Shiva temples have some connection with the Sun.

Vishnu and Shiva connections with the sun are significant for auspicious reasons. Hindu rites generally begin with purification rituals and hence the fire and sun are always significant divinities. The 16th century stone sun image in Panauti, Kavrepalanchok district north of Kathmandu is a striking sculpture. It is near Indreswor Mahadev temple.

The Surya images have various symbolic features in South Asia. Fire has always been the earthly version of the sun in Hindu rituals. This particular connection is chanted in the Rig Veda:

> 6. The birth of the horse is here and in the sun. Guard our patrons from falling prey to malice or injury. When far away in fortresses of unbaked bricks, 8 hatred and false hoods shall not reach him. (p 191, from "2.35 "The Child of the Waters" (Apām Napāt) in *the Rig Veda*).

Doniger explains the slokas[4]:

> Agni is often depicted as a horse, who is in turn identified with the sun; the micro-macrocosmic parallel is enriched by Agni's simultaneous terrestrial and celestial forms, and those of the

---

[4] All citations from *The Rig Veda* are from *Rig Vida, an Anthology*. Trans & Annotations. Wendy Doniger (1981) London: Penguin. Check footnote in the book. Page 194.

waters ('here'). Moreover, the sun, like the child of the waters, is born in the waters.

In "10.190 "Cosmic Heat," the sun is the primordial element or the god created:

> 1. Order and truth were born from heat as it blazed up. From that was born night; from that heat was born billowy ocean.
> 2. From the billowy ocean was born the year, that arranges days and nights, ruling over all that blinks it eyes.
> 3 The Arranger has set in their proper place the sun and moon, the sky and the earth, the middle realm of space, and finally the sunlight.

Furthermore, there is the hymn in the praise of the sun in "1.50 The Sun, Surya":

> 1 His brilliant banners draw upwards the god who knows all creatures, so that everyone may see the sun.
> ...
> 5 You rise up facing all the groups of gods, facing mankind, facing everyone, so that they can see the sunlight.
> ...
> 10 We have come up out of darkness, seeing the higher light around us, going to the sun, the god among gods, the highest light. (359-360)

The *Puranas* may have been composed later than the *Vedas* but there are claims that some of the *Puranas* were composed earlier. The dates of composition cannot be verified without elaborate discourses which I would like to avoid for now.

In Chapter 261 of the *Matsya Purana*, the sage narrator tells that to depict the image of the sun, the artist must present the god as a stable divinity with beautiful eyes and holding lotus in both his hands. The chariot must have seven horses and one wheel. There should be redness emitted by his spectacular mukuta and in the central part of the lotus. He should be decorated with ornaments holding lotuses in both hands. The lotuses should be stylistically elevated above his shoulders. His form, particularly his legs must be embellished by two pieces of clothes. His feet must be dazzling with energy (*tej*). Dandi and Pingal, his associates should be placed on both sides. They should be depicted holding swords. There should be the presence of Dhata or the Brahman holding a pen. The sun god Bhaskar must be surrounded by many divine beings. This is how the image of the sun must be drawn. The charioteer of the sun god is Arun whose complexion should be red like a lotus. [5]

The tradition behind iconographic representation is one of the significant aspects of Hindu devotionalism. The deity has to be visualized in concrete forms. The presence of the body of deity in paintings or sculptures is the appreciation by the viewer. The formless appears as form or the form is the origin of belief and faith which leads to formlessness. Whether the idea comes first or the material is a significant Greek philosophical debate in the lines of Socrates/Plato and Aristotle. The Hindu tradition, whether folk or Vedic, whether folk or Vedic has always realized the significance of form, the very presence of the divinity in icons. The rules of form in art ranges from such Puranic prescriptions to vernacular making a mound of a deity realized in a heap of soil accumulated and made into a sacred space. The forms are rigid as well as loose. But the form exists. The form of the sun god is realized in a chariot-driven act of the rising sun, and at the same time, the sun itself becomes the object of veneration in morning prayer.

---

[5] My translation from Hindi from https://archive.org/details/HindiBookMatsyaPuranByGitaPress/mode/2up

CHAATH

Gaurishwar Bhattacharya writes,

> … the Surya images from southeast of Bangladesh have some iconographic features different from those from the north. The earliest image of the Sun-god is a damged terracotta image from Bogra, now in the Mahasthan Museum. The deity wears a tunic and high boots and a big sword is tied to his waist with a belt. He wears a crown and holds two full-blown lotuses, one in each hand. The image belongs. a crown and holds two full-blown lotuses, one in each hand. The image belongs to the Gupta period. Surya is shown standing in samapada position holding two full-blown lotuses, one in each hand, on a chariot drawn by seven horses. He wears a tall crown, earrings, necklaces, bangles, armlets and a sacred thread (upavita). What is quite striking is that he wears a cuirass (varma) on the chest and high boots. Originally Surya wore a Sassanian dress. The Brhatsamhita describes the early form of Surya, but is silent about the boots. None of the Puranas has any reference to them. (2018: 456)

He writes about the image of the sun god from Deora (Bogra), Rajshahi division in Bangladesh. The high boots resemble Sassanian iconography. The Sassanids were replaced by the Islamic empires. The interconnectedness between the Persian and Indic cultures ranges from iconography to law and strengthened the multicultural nature of Persian and South Asian belief systems.

In *The Markandeya Purana*, the Sun god is mentioned from Canto or *Adhyaya* 102 to 110. In Canto 103. The sage narrator Markandeya speaks about creation by the blessing of the sun:

> Now when the egg was being heated by his glory above and beneath, the lotus born Forefather, being desirous of creating, pondered, "My creation although accomplished will assuredly

pass to destruction through the intense glory of the sun, who is the cause of creation, dessolution and permanence, great of soul. Breathing beings will all be bereft of breath, the waters will dry up through his glory, and without water there will be no creation of the universe." Pondering thus the adorable Brahma, Forefather of the world, becoming intent thereon, composed a hymn to the adorable sun. (556)

The creation thus was unfolded. In Canto 104 Markandeya again speaks:

Having created this world, Brahma then separated off the castes, the brahman's four periods of life, the seas, the mountains, and the islands even as before. The adorable lotus-born god fixed the forms and abodes of the gods, Daityas, Nagas and other beings, as before, according to the Vedas indeed. (559)

In another classical texts, *Brihat Samhita*[6] also known as *Varahmihira Brihat Samhita* by Varahamihira belonging to the 16th century, the sun god is described in various splendor in the six ritus or seasons. In Chapter 3, "The Sun" (ādityacāra) has the following color-splendor:

During Sisira Ritu the colour of the sun will be that of copper of tawny; it will be of greenish yellow or saffron colour in the Vasantha Ritu. It Greeshman Ritu, it will be almost pale or golden; in Varsha Ritu, it will be whitish; in Sharad Ritu, the colour will be that of the interior of the lotus; and in the

---

[6] See *Varahamihira's Brihat Samhita*. Trans. 1946. Panditabhushana V Subramanhaya Sastri. Bangalore: V.B. Soobbiah & Sons. https://archive.org/details/Brihatsamhita/mode/2up

> Hemanta Ritu, it will be blood-red, and the effect on the mankind will be auspicious. In the rainy session, the sun being glossy or showing the colours of other season also is auspicious. (Slokas 23-34)

The appearance of the god is described in Slokas 46-48, Chapter 58, "Descriptions of Idols."[7]

> The sun-god's nose, forehead, shanks, thighs, cheeks and breast should be elevated; he should be dressed in the northern style, covering the body from breast to foot. He holds two lotuses born of his hands, in his arm; bears a diadem; his face is adorned with ear-rings, he a a pear-neckless and a girdle round her waste. His face has the luster of the interior of the lotus; his body is covered with an armor; face, pleasant with a smile and a halo bright with gems (or circle of bright lusters of gems). Such a sun is auspicious for the architect. (Slokas 46-48)

In Slokas 49-52, the height for the image of the sun is prescribed for various purposes and it also mentions suffering if the image is made erroneously.

Some of the major texts which refer to the sun god are in *Chandogya Upnishad*, the fifth century and extensively revised text *Bhavisya Purana*, the pre-Christian or medieval text[8] *Brhad-devata*, and Telgu text *Brahmana Sarvasva*.

Saurya (the sun) sect was popular in Gupta period in India. Persian tradition of sun worship, of Mithra has connections with Vedic tradition of the worship of Hindu deity Mitra, one of the

---

[7] See p. 514 from *Vrahamihira Brihat Samhita*.

[8] There are controversies regarding the dating of the text which ranges from pre-Christian times to the 11th century A.D.

The sacral

Adityas, the twelve celestial beings in Hindu pantheon. Among the Indian cities, Mathura was a site of sun cult, writes Dr. Suresh Pandey[9]. The other famous shrines of the Sun in India are 8th century A. D. Martand Sun temple, some four to five miles from Anantanag, Kashmir, the tenth century A. D. Modhera Sun temple in Gujarat made by the Chalukyas, and the thirteenth century Konarak Sun temple in Orissa are the significant sites. In the paintings in Singanpur, Rajsthan, the sun emits seven rays. Similarly, in Sita Kondi, Chambal Valley, Madhyapradesh, the image of the sun is in full radiance (Shantilal Nagar: 1998: 118). Nagar writes about the Indus Valley Chanhudaro sun image:

---

[9] See "Solar Iconography of Mathura" in Pandey, S. (1999). SOLAR ICONOGRAPHY OF MATHURA. *Proceedings of the Indian History Congress, 60*, 1097-1103. Retrieved July 31, 2021, from http://www.jstor.org/stable/44144184

CHAATH

These very striking sun motifs, which were so popular with the people of Chanhudaro and are so abundantly seen the pottery from the site, are not represented in Mohenjodaro and rarely occur on the wares of the contemporary date from other excavated Harappan sites. They take various form and position on the pottery. Especially prominent specimens are available on shreds and its use as a repetition motif in wider borders is also available. The center of the device is either a plain circle with a spot in the middle or an annulus divided into four quarters each on of which is filled-in with some form of ornamentation. The rays issuing from the center may be either straight with oblique ends or set at a tangent, the last being by far the most common. Each ray terminates in a leaf like form, pipal leaves having been used. This combination of plant form and orb perhaps symbolizes the close connection between vegetation and sunshine … (119).

Chaath is a continuation of the wider South Asian art and rituals of the sun, from Indus Valley roots to the poetic traditions of the *Vedas*. The traces of art and ritual have always been in the village imaginations of the South Asian cultures which the Vedic pantheon may have borrowed because the agrarian cultures predate the rise of Vedic period.

The initiation of the sun ritual and the worship of Chaath mother connects the agrarian with the sky, the earth with the sun. Along with the earth and the sun, the water association symbolizes the three most vital life sources for the living beings. The performances are conducted by women, and perhaps one of the most popular festivals in vast region which does not see the male participation in any significant ways.

CONCLUSION
Trees, Animals, Anthropocentric Humans and Post-humans

Festivals in Nepal are associated with animals and trees like in many of the Hindu and Buddhist festivals in South Asia. I seek to conceptualize the natural objects and human relationship within the double bind of anthropocentrism and post-humanism both as humans becoming technological beings as well as critiquing their identities as humanists. I will also discuss how myths in form of rituals pay respect to animals despite their teleological motives.

We may believe that humans live by memory and trees do not. But trees contain circles of memory within themselves. The rings formed in a tree not only tell its age but in many cases tell the environmental conditions of the time. Trees notified that AD 536 in Europe was extremely environmentally abnormal year of cold. Dendrochronology, by observing the rings of pine and oak trees, found that there were abnormal little growths inside the rings during AD 536. The history is hidden in the rings of memory.

We can take the example of photosynthesis too. Neither photosynthesis is memory nor a humanly understood rational act but these plants and trees act with senses of survival and records of how environment behaved in the evolutionary tale of the earth.

Photosynthesis is the food making process of a plant through its green leaves. Chlorophyll is the green pigment in the leaves which is the kitchen oven of the entire process. Chlorophyll takes the sun light, carbon dioxide from the air and water from roots to make food, which is glucose or starch, and supplies to the entire plant for its growth. But photosynthesis as by product emits oxygen and water molecules in the atmosphere. But the making of food is a complex process which occurs inside the leaf.

A leaf has a wider part called lamina, a large surface to absorb the sun light. In the cross section of a leaf, there are closely sequenced cells. These cells have chloroplast which contain the pigments Chlorophyll providing green color to the leaf. There are tiny channels which absorb water into the leaves. Stomata in the lower section in general absorb carbon dioxide from the air. Water and Carbon dioxide inter into Chlorophyll and thus they are finally absorbed into the chloroplast which trap energy from the sun light. The energy synthesizes glucose and oxygen from Carbon dioxide and water. These oxygen and glucose molecules diffuse out of the chloroplast. Glucose then is transported with the help of channels to all parts of the plant; oxygen is diffused out into atmosphere out of the stomata which earlier during the photosynthesis had absorbed carbon dioxide from the atmosphere but now gives oxygen.

I have obviously not introduced any new idea about rings and photosynthesis but have revisited the processes the plants lives are involved in. I have not imparted any new knowledge to the reader but have merely described the process to remind us about the complexity of nature and its growth. How complex and dynamic their living processes are and how anthropomorphic attitudes have constantly disregarded other lives. The growth of the human rational mind is a tiny part of evolutionary history. Millions have evolved and perished in the planetary history and there are millions who have survived for eons.

No photosynthesis no food chain. Animals depend on the plant for its fruit, for clean air, and for multiple survivals: the chain is immense from the corner of your garden to Amazon forest. The

CONCLUSION

'food', the energy is circulated (food chain) in the sets of condition like in Chitwan forest[1] is a matter of supporting life (ecosystem). When it is interrupted by artificial human means disasters unfold. The food and the system is the complex set of processes which humans have the capacity to ignore because he thinks that the cosmic movement up in the sky and nature below is for him. We all know what rings or a tree and photosynthesis in the leaves are.

This is the complexity of survival which goes on from tiny plants to massive Bunyan trees. The complexity of life is all around us, visible and invisible. Who is the plant helping then? 'For itself and in the process the humans' is a mindless thought. It is as senseless to claim that the stars by being constellations are moving for us, and only for us, not for a fly, and also for me as a Hindu or differently for a Christian next door, or for a Christian only.

The stars up there, millions and billions of light year away do not exist for us signaling grace and curse. Their rays and gravitational forces determine good and bad time, the astrologer would claim with unfounded and unscientific constructions. They do not exist for our astrological teleology. Down here on the earth, plants do not work for themselves but in the very "relative chance for survival" as Loren Eiseley writes (2008: 138). They live and let others live, not humans but with the unconscious bonding from the sky to the earth. It is not merely survival through photosynthesis but for contingency of survival, the survival for relationality where acts of human make things catastrophic. Reminding us of photosynthesis and many such deliverances of the plants and animals is ethical humility, not merely teaching one of photosynthesis but realizations of how complex a tree is and how it works for survival in the precarious conditions of life and death of species.

---

[1] We have visited Chitwan area with Shankar Paudel at many times to conduct research on rivers and seasons. Shankar in a doctoral student at UTEP.

The Essence of Love

Biophilous sentiment in humans or the habit to love is as primordial as the first microbs of evolution is. Love for life in the plants is as old as life on the earth. How do we value such love? By the ritual like tree worship? It may be one of the most significant ways of venerating and preserving nature despite the fact that these festivals have anthropomorphic ideologies. Tree worship is a humble example in Hindu and Buddhist traditions and also in European and African ethnic practices, and world around.

Worshipping a dog for a day or feeding the crow is the symbolic act of love; "I learnt it with my mother during *Kaag Tihar*, once a year in my childhood, then one day a teacher explained to us in the class about the complex system of photosynthesis, I wondered - preparing notes and happening to look outside my window, a crow sharing crumbs of bread with other crows, the food my mother had left on the terrace - if a leaf works so calmly to cook silently, how does these crows work. I started feeding them every day. I asked my mother why didn't she teach me to feed not only during the festival but daily. She replied, it should have come to you naturally." He was my student. The symbolic act of creation in the midst of our survival is the simple act of knowing how others struggle to survive.

CONCLUSION

The piping notes of eagle sounds to me like singing up in the blue. The buzzing of bees in the hives is like the thousand notes corresponding to the hissing of snakes – buzzing and hissing are the closet tonal harmony to unnerve you, one scares you and the other terrifies you. Unlearn the fear and one may find the rhythms in their music. Cicadas chirp, a constant sound of very delicate rising and falling tones: its chirping is different from that of crickets. Strangely complementing the buzzing and hissing. They all are singing in the symbolic act of creation. Why symbolic? It is because we have to understand them; they are not given to us to understand by our senses.

How ready we are to apply our sensory perception to understand the world of insects, birds, and animals[2]. Our movement with the cultural baggage are generally obstacles to understand the world of nature. Why does a bird sing? When is an elephant calmly resting, when is a monkey suspicious, a rhino agitated, a tiger aggressive, or a snake defensive. A cockroach does not generally fly away if you blow air for the second time but flies do. A pigeon can fly back to the same spot even after leaving it hundreds of miles away, a honeybee has the ability to remember its route. Their sensory experiences are vital for humans to understand by human sensory responses. Tiger is a shy animal and unless it encounters a human directly, eye to eye, it may not be dangerous. We keep domestic animals in a cultural space, outside the forest. But the least interfered space, the deeper forest is always a space of the unknown even to a seasoned zoologist[3].

---

[2] Shankar Paudel is working with me on this area of animal comprehensive behavior. He is a researcher in South Asian Foundation for Academic Research (SAFAR).

[3] In our research team, Shankar along with Renuka Khatiwada, Khagendra Nepal, and Sedu Dhakal's artistic and performative works has been talking to the people and experts for a long time

The closest sensory experience with the domestic animals is tactual which is remotely possible with wild animals. The case in point is that the tactual experience is out of the question in the wild. The forest is an alien space to modern humans. Crossing the buffer stripe is the most responsible human act which is very easily ignored[4].

Canopy and understory sections of forest trees and the concentration of light that varies and along with shade-tolerant plants, and the insects that live in the logs and woods are not exposed to aliens beyond it habitat neighbors. There are more insects in canopy than in understory in tropical forests[5]. The sunflecks determine how these life forms are distributed. My argument rests on how we inter into a forest or interact with animals. Humans inter for fodder, hunting, and touristic entertainments. Walking too is a daily activity in and around forest areas. How much silence and sound we emit or do not emit depends on where we are in the forest and how we use our senses to act or not to act.

Human behavior with intense sensory application is vital (failure is fatal in multiple terms) when elephants are in heat. Their aggression is on its peak and a slight infringement by the norms of human behavior in the forest brings catastrophic consequences. When and how to comprehend such animal behavior is the matter of how to distinguish Ghariyals which are less aggressive from Magar crocodiles. Another human sensory perception is significant

---

[4] The elephant safari in Chitawn is the most disturbing human interference in the forest area. The mahuts and tourists talk and shout constantly during jungle safaris.

5 Preisser, Evan, David C. Smith and Margaret D. Lowman Selbyana. (1998). "Canopy and Ground Level Insect Distribution in a Temperate Forest" Vol. 19, No. 2, CANOPY PROCEEDINGS (1998), pp. 141-146 (6 pages) Published By: Marie Selby Botanical Gardens Inc. https://www.jstor.org/stable/41759984

CONCLUSION

to be acted upon is to understand the nature of resting animals. Birds and aquatic living forms are more incomprehensive than the animals like elephants, beers, rhinos, lions, tigers, and deer.

Such interactions demand highest level of sensibility towards wild animals. The same level of sensibility is equally significant when we behave with the domesticated animals which are in our company. Humans domesticate animals for meat to milk, for sacrifices and redemption. Animals are acted upon for many such purposes. Tribal religious and scriptural norms are mostly anthropocentric when it comes to sacrifices though devotion and worship have elements of faith and honesty that the flesh pleases the deities. We have multiple ideas and attitudes to answer the question what the role of religious rituals is toward the animals we need for our purpose.

What is the role of technology, cybernetics towards animals while human is rethought and reconfigured in post-human modes? Human is not merely biological entity but a bionics in post-human recognition. An advanced post-human bio-techno configuration of the human may have responded better to the onslaught of the Covid-19 virus: we do not know. We are not yet post-human in Dona Haraway's "we are cyborg" claim when one traces the under privileged humanity from islands to continents. The human survival is at stake due to climate change and the serge of viruses. The question of animals and their survival and our attitude towards them are still the same: to consume either by sacrificial rituals or through KFCization. Despite post-human identity is not entirely fictional, the question may be pertinent: what is the role of post-humans toward animals? We may find agency in this new urbanized western role (Haraway's cyborg is a hastily done urban claim of a few) but what does post-human see about the assault on animals from the quarters of religion and consumer market? In some ways, in ironically distinct ways, the modern medicine made out of animal parts to experimentation have have been instrumental in making humans post-human but human attitudes and beliefs are the same, the blood on the alter and the flesh in the kitchen. So what does this evolving new human think about animals. I will try to trace some answers soon. The issue I deal with for a while is what post-human studies study animals in the last fifty or so years.

The investments to study animals has been unprecedented in the later half of the twentieth century. Humberto Maturana is an exemplary neurophysiologist from Chile who worked on frogs to explain how a frog sees the world from his observational point of view. The frog sees the flies to construct its reality and sees the flowing objects which it wants to eat and not the big animals passing by. His theory of autopoiesis is the construction of reality by what the animals want to construct. Humans are not different in their cultural contexts: they construct religiosity of eating and not eating cow. We are not different than frogs because we consider meat as goat or chicken, beef not lamb, lamb not beef, and not dogs not chimpanzees. Frogs are different because they create reality by reflexes as Maurana would suggest but humans construct reality by rational thinking. Autopoiesis is self production of reality, a constructed agency, a world understood by perspectives. In the process of construction, the role of the senses weaken: intellect

I too Worship for food

CONCLUSION

overpower intuition. We are rational and thus we are noisy, loud, arrogant.

Human noise is the most hazardous factors in the natural world. Tourism has added to such noises. The touristic elephant rides in the jungle are noisy, crowded, and painful to the wild in the forest. The invading noises of human intrusion into the forests have been of less concern in Nepali natural parks either for touristic purposes or for the lack of scientific studies to empower what is right and what is wrong. African jungle safaris are the most visible cultured sin acted upon the calmness of animal world. Humans are endowed with scientific knowledge which has glorified our knowledge and our place in the world. Science has its ignorance as religion has. Both are ignorant toward myth.

One problem with science is the ignorance toward myth. What myth does and what religion prescribes are different. Mythical consciousness has come to humans as residues of thoughts and memories from thousands of years (I am reminded of Carl Jung's racial memory[6]). If killing is the teleological ingredient of both myth and religion, mythic perception of killing has the element of innocence. Killing is for survival, for pleasing the angry deity. Religious institutionalization too practices killing for pleasing the deities but is more normative than spontaneous, more prescriptive than natural. Scientific approach to myth needs to look at the differences between myth and religion despite their deep associations and ritualistic overlapping. Myth, in my conceptualization, is half of the city not religion. And the role of the animals and plants are very significant in this visuality of 'the half of the city'. Myths are gone, the cities turn 'smart'.

---

[6] See in Bibliography of Works Cited. Carl Jung. *The Archetypes and the Collective Unconscious.*

Setting in Silence

    Myth is imperative to be human, modern human, post-human. The primacy of mythic response to natural world were awe, fear, excitement, reverence and many such emotional spontaneities. The Neolithic cultures' interaction to natural phenomena had multiple perceptions from knowing the surrounding, explaining it in supernatural terms as something more powerful than them, hence imagining magic in nature, and being normative that there are some rules to follow to be at par with the erratic nature. Animals beings are different to homo sapiens in many respects were considered either as their associates or as part of nature, or even part of supernatural. What mythic consciousness does with animals is with commitments of love or hate: friend or enemy, domestic or wild. Thus animals are equal to humans in mythic awareness. With animals, humans competed, fought, conquered, defeated, befriended, chased and being chased and moved ahead in the phases of evolution: a Nietzschean version of "the will to power."

    The 'civilized' humans, the humans of their own histories, whether humanist humans or the post-humans have less the spark to compete with animals; humans conquer the animals, use them,

CONCLUSION

kill them, and domesticate them. When myth becomes merely fictional and superstitious by the modern mind, there evolutionary story turns anthropocentric constructs of man and the other, the other as animals, land, water, and forest.

Through rituals the valley culture retains the mythic consciousness though in ambivalent terms. There is no rationality to defend the rituals of sacrifice but in the same seasons of the divine, the dogs and crows become as sacred as cows are, the animal-faced deities are blood soaked and, at the same time, are the deities of knowledge and protector-mothers.

The myth of crow and dog are the last remnants in the rituals. Animals are protected in reservations as trees are. Once the monstrosities of industrialization rampages the forests, the culture of progress becomes the culture of killing. In my school days, I always wondered how the great ancient civilizations turned into deserts. Despite being creative in the arts and progressive in development, they now are the ruins of their former glories. I now understand when I observe the destruction of nature in the best of the developmental psyche, why they fell and how we too will fall. We are the fools of the most bizarre kinds: we claim that the global warming is a hoax.

Rice Plantation, Kathmandu

Aesthetics: The Symmetry of Senses

Our expressions, at times, become art and art acts upon one special thing very meticulously: expressions are given shapes, given forms. This is the idea of aesthetics from formalistic point of view where the form can be understood as, for instance, color, lines, shape, proportion, texture, image, and symbol. Aesthetics is also about pleasure and delight, which evolves out of how art represents reality and affects our sensibilities, our emotions and feelings, by the use of colors, light and shade, lines and contours, to stimulate the senses of the viewer. Along with these aspects of aesthetics, nostalgia, memory and narrative are also aesthetics which art evokes. In the nativity painting of Buddha[7] the images appear through, for instance, colors and lines creating order and balance and at the same time it unfolds a narrative of miracle, memories of identities, cultures, and belongings to ancientness.

I focus on art as form and how form leads to concepts with our intense participation with them. This is a significant mode of understanding aesthetics. Form can be understood through harmony or arrangement of parts in the painting which appeals to our senses like the central Buddha figure walking on the lotus flower is flanked by natural and supernatural elements; walking Buddha figure and the surrounding elements create harmony. The two sides of the painting with Buddha in the middle reveal arrangement. There are Mayadevi, mother of Buddha, and a female attendant on the right and the full blossomed tree that the mother is holding. On the left, there are deities descending down from and with the clouds to bless the baby Buddha, already transformed Siddhartha as Buddha by the very act of miraculous walk. It is the beginning of

---

[7] see the image in https://commons.wikimedia.org/wiki/File:Birth_of_Buddha_at_Lumbini.jpg

CONCLUSION

walk, the first steps which is going to define the course of history of suffering and nirvana. While the baby walks, both the figures on the right and left, the greenish color on the right and bluishness on the left give the sense of arrangement of one color leading to another.

Furthermore, form is also about the order the visual creates: the lotus path which Buddha walks becomes the order in the painting as well as prophecy of walk in the history to come. If the path organizes the images in the painting an order can be conceived; the path is the ordering factor because of its present supernatural walk just after the birth as Sidhartha and equally superhuman dimension of walk as Buddha in future. The future is suggestive of the history to unfold. 'Sidhartha who takes steps is Buddha who walks' is one of the two stabilizing factors in the painting connecting the present and the future.

Mayadevi appears as the dominant central figure with her right hand gesturing affectionately. If the path is the ordering element,

A courtyard in Patan

the mother controls the harmony and order which are visible in the painting.

Along with aesthetics as form, I mentioned that there is a significant aspect of aesthetics with narrative: what narrative does one imagine after seeing an image? One of the most revealing photographs is Renuka Khatiwada's "My Ornaments, My Nemesis," which was exhibited at Premier University in Chittagong in 2018. Sadat Khan who wrote on her collection of photographs titles his work as "Chittagong Symphony" which discourses the very narrative from the materiality of the picture. The photograph narrates the economic history of the sea port. The evening sets in and the lighted ships move in the Karnaphuli river. The ships are like the ornaments in the darkening evening sky and yet they are the agents of progress for the city and still disastrous for the pristine nature that the river once was. The progress of the city is disaster for the river, hence her ornaments (the ships which look colorfully beautiful) are also the nemeses for nature, the river. The story of the river and the ships is a long story of the city. Seeing the ships floating on the chest of the river in the photograph, the memory of the river bank glides when, says an academic of the English Department at Premier University, *adda*[8] used to be around the impending crisis with hope and nervousness when the revolution was declared in Chittagong. It was not like normal *adda* but gathering for future directions. "Karnaphuli seemed to me like a mother and I still get overwhelmed when I see the bank where I used to sit with friends."

---

[8] *Adda* in Bengali is a casual sitting and chatting sessions in the evening with friends in neighborhood corners, fields, tea stalls and at many such places. *Adda* culture is one of the features of Bengali cities and towns. Nepali version of adda could be realized during the mid eighties at Pipal Bot, Kathmandu when people used gather and spent time in the evening. I even remember even Ganesh Man Singh, a towering political leader, used to come and spend time with his acquaintances.

CONCLUSION

The aesthetics of the form and its symbolic comprehension is best understood in the philosophic rendering of Milan Ratna Shakya. The symbol the work of art, the Mandala, represents, is for me the aesthetic dimension because Shakya's interpretation and understanding of the Mandala is based on the visuality of the art. He conceives the Mandala in these modes of internalization. He considers it as the symbol to reach from one state of consciousness to the other: as "Buddo-Hindu ceremonial nebula," the form that leads to "higher awareness," "secured status of oneness with the void '*Śūñya*' as the infinite spirit … " (2017: *Mandala*: 1-2); as a circuit where each day is conceived as a new beginning: "Symbolism of life cycle as to be predicted by reading a horoscope chart," as "a life … perceived in a circuit of cosmic elements, like water, earth, fire, wind and atmosphere," "as beginning of … origin of life as creation of the world to celebrate each day as new and birthday with rotation as a Mandalic calendar …" (2-3); as bliss or Buddhahood: as '*Abhiṣeka*', 'coronation' to aspire in baptism of the esoteric realms," in "'the paradise of Buddha, '*Buddhakṣetra*', "five brooding Buddhas,"

Pimbahal Pokhari (Pond) in Patan

"Buddhist sacred realm as cause and effect of Mandala" (3-4). Thus, for Shakya, the Mandala represents a higher state of mind, lifecycle, and bliss. It is the aesthetic comprehension of the Mandala, as a pure form as linear (vertically from lower to higher), circular (life as cyclical), and point (the ultimate blissfulness) respectively.

Newar epistemology conceives the Mandala as pure form which the valley is as the representation of consciousness, circularity, and blissfulness. The liturgical aspect is the colorfulness which the Mandala represents and which the valley is in its multiple dimensions with people and places, music and architecture. The form thus conceives the city, or the city is the form. The city is a constant movement within seasons with art, performances, and rituals.

Another aspect of form can be constantly seen in the temples and images all around. The city itself is a *mudra* with its abundant icons. Shakya reminded me that *mundra* is *charitra* or characteristic: iconography thus requires a systematic and appropriate understanding of images.

> In Nepal, interesting material for the study of Buddhist iconography is obtained from an entirely unexpected quarter. There is a class of people called the Citrakāras or professional artists. They are so proficient in their art that they can produce an excellent drawing of any Buddhist deity in a few minutes. These artists seem to have a phenomenal memory with regard to the iconographic details such as the number of faces and hands, the pose, the symbols, the weapons and the parental Dhyāni Buddha. They prepare such drawings in the presence of the customer without ever referring to a book or painted specimen, although at home they keep albums full of drawings in black and white and paintings in colour all relating to Buddhist deities. (Binoytosh: 1958: 7)

My Ornaments, My Nemesis

Why is form important to understand narrative with memory and transform that in art? Why do we need to comprehend the philosophy behind the story?

There is a brilliant tradition in Bhaktapur, I understood how a guru tells stories to the artists from Buddhist Sutras and Hindu epics. After listening to the story by the guru-narrator the artists understand the content of the story, they first draw sketches and then sculpt and paint. The characteristic which appears in an image has this holistic comprehension of a story with memory to transform the story into art. The idea is how the form of emotion is concretized in images by the artist after going through a readerly experience of the narratives. The iconography is the form which evolves from the the story, the characteristic which the *mudra* captures. *Mudra* is the visual comprehension of the feature of the image.

Emotions tamed in art as accomplishments transforms an event of killing into narrative, it is the taming of the horrible which art does, Nietzsche tells us many a times. The emotion of anger is tamed into deeds and full of horror though. For instance, referring to Durga and Mahisasura image in Bhaktapur Durbar square, I talk in my documentary "Anger and the Mahatma" that one can see

> that this is the moment of death blow by a deity of cosmic proportion to an equally powerful demon, Mahishasura. The goddess is piercing her lance into the chest of the evil incarnate.[9] Her anger disguised or is it the eternal smile of rage! Is she looking at a distance while killing the demon because the evil is insignificant? Why is she in a meditative detachment away from the target? Why is the target not targeted? The lance pierces the chest of the demon who looks helpless while she smiles looking elsewhere… The victor is not angry and the vanquished is not in terror but in a posture of compassionate sublime. Is he stupefied by the indifferent look of the goddess? The ultimate moment of death is the moment of union of the evil with the supernatural? How is anger displayed in this mythical image representing the narrative of the war of Durga and Mahishasura? (Arun Gupta: 2021)

The image at the Durbar Square corresponds to the story which leads to artistic interpretation of the anger as acceptance of the evil into godhood. Since there is the lance which pierces the demon, the aspect of anger cannot be ignored. Anger thus is framed, as I narrate, as meditative detachment. An artist captures the essence of rage which is the goddess looking away from the target.

Similarly, there is the anger of Bhim while killing Dushashana and Draupadi's calm after she wets her hair with the blood of the enemy. The artistic captures the essence of two sets of anger when

---

[9] As narrated in many Hindu narratives and more specially in the *Markandeya Purana*. The Puranas are the compendia of stories about creation, gods and goddesses, about morals, evils and the ways of the world.

he or she comprehends the story from the epic relating the part to the whole. I present in the documentary:

> There is another dimension of celebration? You kill and avenge and I will wet and tie my hair with the blood of my arch-enemy. My decades of loosened locks will I tie and I will avenge the humiliation by his blood. Draupadi has taken this vow.
> The mythical epical hero of the *Mahabharata*, Bhim tears away the chest of Dushashana and takes the blood out to wet the unfastened locks of Draupadi who had promised to tie her hair only if Bhim kills Dhushashana. Previously, Dushashana had dragged her from her room to the court, mortifying her in front of the male gathering of the heroes of the clan. She had pleaded that she was in a menstrual phase. Yudhisthara had lost his property, his kingdom, his brothers, and Draupadi to the prince Duryodhana in a game of dice.
> Bhim's anger is expressed as extreme form of aggression. Draupadi's deep breath seeing the blood in Bhim's cupped hands is aggression as calming effect. The blood cools her anger of being dragged disheveled, half nude in the court. (2021)

Extreme form of Bhim's anger is not that of Draupadi's anger as calming down: there is a continuum of anger, not different but not similar expressions of emotion. Bhim annihilates the enemy and Draupadi welcomes the hero; there is continuity of one form of anger leading to another. The art (acting) in my documentary captures the story. Anger is tamed into the power of annihilation of the evil and readiness to realize that the killing is accomplished.

The form is the visual in front of us. The visual is everywhere in Newar cultural spaces from rituals to paintings, dance to dramas. The visual speaks through its forms, the form as color, line, light, depth, and images. The visual is pervasive through rituals and festivals which are the aspects of realization of the divine. The idea of visual is one of the significant aspects of internalizing the world and what we may understand by philosophy. In its cognitive sense, the self revelation or annunciation within is *darshan* in Sanskrit which implicitly connotes to the term philosophy; it is the love of wisdom for the ancient Greeks. Philosophy generally is related with the questions of knowing and existence. The search for knowing what creation, universe, nature, god, humans, animals and so on are. To know is epistemological concern of philosophy. On the other hand, the inquiries about being or existence are metaphysical or ontological concerns. The inquiries of knowing and being are not separate: these quests always complement one another. We generally learn, communicate and understand the matters of knowing and being through the medium of the verbal language. We write about them, we speak and we exchange ideas. We use the verbal language to express ourselves and listen to others, their ideas or concepts.

There is another complementary domain that we use to communicate: we exchange our ideas with the help of visual language too. The term *darshan* implies expressing, seeing or visualizing ideas. The term *darshan* suggest that understanding can be achieved through visual language too. Understanding is both verbal and visual; *darshan* encompasses both verbal and visual understandings. In ancient South Asian tradition, the men of wisdom were called *seers* (*drasta* in Sanskrit). For instance, an allegory from the ancient myths is about the idea of visuality and cognition or visuality as cognition. The celebrated *mantra* Gayatri was revealed as an idea to Vishwamitra, the mythical sage of the Hindus. The implication is that he could see the mantra, the idea of the mantra, so profoundly that it manifested itself into an appearance, as the goddess. The idea for him was a vision, a revelation, visuality. Seeing is to transform ideas into physical perception or visual understanding. There is another allegory from the epic *Mahabharata*. The famous mythical story of Yashoda seeing the cosmos in her baby Krishna's mouth is an appropriate anecdote to understand the term *darshan*. One

CONCLUSION

fine day she forced the baby's mouth open to check whether he had stolen some curd or not, she finds nothing and yet everything. She suddenly sees the entire cosmos inside his mouth. The infinite compassion of the mother envisioned her associate the son with the universe. The act of seeing the world in the mouth is seeing everything in the son or the son being everything for the mother. The symbolic significance of the myth is more important than believing or disbelieving the story. The narration reveals that it was the moment of *darshan*: the mother's affection toward the son, a time of sublime visualizing and thus suggesting the meaning of love in visual terms. The modern allegory is equally comprehensible: once Albert Einstein told about the Scot physicist James Clerk Maxwell that when the later was working on his theories, he would imagine himself riding through space, so to speak, astride a light wave and look back at the wave next to him.

Visualization is the evocation of the inner eye. The inner eye requires the intensity, an approach to understanding things around. Visualization is about concentration. Visualization is not merely looking at things, it is perceiving objects and ideas with the fullest of participation of the senses. Thus the word *darshan* has this visual perceptual connotation and conceptual understanding.

The visual concentration on form to read the icons is the most significant aspect to understand the artistic dimension of the valley. Min Bahadur Shakya in *The Iconography of Nepalese Buddhism* has provided an interpretive look on the aspects of form and how they lead to the meaning of the images. The relation between Buddha images as mimetic modes of Buddha. The ideas are concretized: scriptures are the manifestations of Dharma, and Sangha is represented by Boddhisastwas and Bhikshus. Furthermore, the objects of inner refuge are Gurus, Istadevas, and Dakinis (22). The idea of "Buddham saranam gacchami, Dhamam saranam gacchami, Sangham saranam gacchami" takes the form of the Buddha images, the scriptures, and the collectivity of people. The concept of visualization of the idea has been the core of South Asian art and religion. The valley in particular has a strong presence of the relationship of forms (Buddha images, Scriptures, and collectivity of people) and the ideas (Buddha, Dharma, and Sangha[10]). The relation between the form and meaning: Milan Ratna Shakya emphasizes that "enlightenment exists with no icon for meditation" (2017: 26). He explains that *rupa* is a visual form (26). He elaborates:

> It is focused in revelation of knowledge. Rupa strings in creation of core object. It decodes in art to imply all creative nature in pubescent creatures. Rupa relates in tangible concept of form out of intangible speculation of any philosophical object, Thus, any kind of object occupy a form, volume and dimension in space. It embraces all manifested forms as visible to this world. (26)

The relationship of form and meaning, rupa and concept is a bondage which is necessary to understand the artistic world of the valley.

The Mahayana concept Buddha who appears to the believers have three forms which is known as *Trikaya*. The believer envisions

---

[10] Gurus, Istadevas, and Dakinis are the deities of inner refuge in the Sangha. Dakinis are obviously representatives of Sangha in the inner refuge. They are peaceful as well as wrathful. They wear bone ornaments. Some are in dancing posture. Some are even nude. These Dakinis generally travel through empty space hence also called Sky-goers. They help the practitioners by eliminating different obstacles and by guiding to realization of the path to enlightenment. They are able to grant eight great powers (skt. astasiddhi) to all devoted practitioners. Some Dakinis are animal faced like Simhavaktra (lion-faced), Vajravarahi (sow-faced), Sardulamukha (tiger-faced) and many others. Vajrayogini is said to be Sarva-Buddha Dakini who confers Buddhahood to the practitioners. These Buddha Dakinis are said to be the representatives of Wisdom or Prajna-paramita. (Min Bahardur Shakya 31-32)

CONCLUSION

Buddha at his/her level of understanding, or more particularly, his or her growth of the self at spiritual level. Nirmankaya is the very immediate understanding of Buddha: Buddha in this state is the apparitional body. This form gives impetus to another form called Smabhogakaya, the body of the enjoyment. Min Bahadur Shakya writes:

> According to Tantric Buddhist tradition, all Buddhas like Vajradhara, Vajrasattva and Yidam deities appear in the form of Sambhogakaya. They have all sorts of ornaments and garments signifying the qualities of enlightenment. The multi-arm, multi-face and multi-emblems they hold are the embodiments of the qualities of enlightenment. (1994: 31)

The writer emphasizes: "In Sambhogakaya there is no limit of capacity or ability of his body …" (31). The limitlessness brings sexuality as the embodiment of higher realization instead of conceiving it as something degradingly mundane. Deities like Vajradhara, Vajrasattva and Yidam deities appear in the form of Sambhogakaya.

The Sacred Walk

Their ornaments signify the virtues of enlightenment (31). The embellishment associated with multiple such images are the forms to comprehend Buddha in the modalities of Trikaya.

Istadevatas i.e. Yidam Herukas, writes Shakya,

> are depicted in their Sambhogakaya aspects. Their specific color, emblems, faces are the metaphorical ways of expressing the qualities of enlightenment. For example 16-armed Mahakala represents the deity indicating 16 types of emptiness he represents. Four-armed Mahakala represents his dominion over four Maras, the (four obstructions on the path of Enlightenment). Yamantaka, who kills the Lord of death, represents the deathlessness aspect of perfect enlightenment. (32)

Istadevatas or Yidam are the deities of the mind: they represent what the mind manifests in various level of realizations. For instance, Hevajra, Cakrasamvara, Kalacakra are the Yidams who function as the mental categories of realization. They are Sambhogakaya Buddhas. They are also manifested in sexual images: the fearsome and the erotic are the mental bond which is metaphoric as defiance to binaries. Cakrasamvara[11] is the most revered of Yidam deities. Kalachakra[12] is an equally venerated deity in Vajrayana tradition.

---

[11] Cakrasamvara in this form is deep blue in colour. He has four faces. The front face is blue-black, right face is white, back face is yellow, his left face is red. He is in ecstatic union with his consort Vajravarahi, red in colour. (Min Bahadur Shakya 152)

[12] Kalacakra has four faces, twenty-four arms and two legs. His front face is blue with bare fans, right face is read, left white and rear yellow each with three eyes. His blue face expresses wrathfulness. The deity is adorned with many jewel. (146) The consort of Kalacakra is called Visvamati. She is yellow in

CONCLUSION

The Yidam deity Hevjra and Vajravarahi, similarly, represent Sambhogakaya.

Finally, the truth of Buddhahood comes to complete comprehension with Dharmakaya or Dharma body. Buddha is realized as Tathata or suchness, the ultimate truth called Buddhahood which at times understood as the Vajra and as the center of the Mandala.

Min Bahadur Shakya writes:

> According to Vajrayana tradition, this wisdom of Dharmakaya is classified into five wisdoms i.e. all pervasive wisdom, mirror-like wisdom, wisdom of equality, discriminative wisdom and all-accomplishing wisdom. This five forms of wisdom [is] represented by five transcendental Buddhas called Vairocana, Akshobhya, Ratna Sambhava, Amitabha and Amogha Siddhi. (29)

The five Taras[13], the consorts of the Dhyani Buddhas represent the wisdom accordingly:

---

colour and has four faces each with three eyes. The other three faces are white, black and red. She has eight arms, four each on the either side. The first right hand embraces Kalacakra, the second a vajra hook, the third a damaru, and the fourth a rosary. 148

[13] Arya Tara is sometimes regarded as Green Tara and personified with Bhrikuti, the historical princess of Nepal who was married to a Tibetan king. White Tara (consort of Virochana) evolves out of the compassion of Avalokitesvara. Ekajata Tara is the terrible form of Akshobhya. The reference to their characterization are based on Min Bahadur Shakya and David Kinsley's (1998). *Tantric Visions of the Divine Feminine: The Ten Mahavidyas*. Delhi: Motilal Banarasidass.

Vajradhateswari (Virochana) represents absolute wisdom and the color is white

Lochana (Akshobya) represents mirror wisdom and the color is blue

Mamki (Ratna Sambhava) represents equalizing wisdom and the color is yellow

Padmani (of Amitava) represents discriminating wisdom and the color is red

Arya Tara (Amogha Siddhi) represents accomplishing wisdom and the color is green

The dominance of color with the attributes of various mode of wisdom is conceptualizing the deity as knowledge through the visibility of colors. Color is traditionally used as the sensa to evoke aesthetic response to the nature of the goddess in various forms or the color places the deity into various attributes.

The visibility is the symmetry of the senses from our understanding of the nativity image of Buddha, the Mandala to colors of wisdom in the Taras. Any such image, temple, monument in the cities of the valley are to be experienced by walking into the premises, by the materiality of what is in front of us.

When the concrete is visualization of the concept – concrete as the form – the aesthetics connects the form and the idea. This is how the visual perception or the use of sense produce the symmetry to represent idea. The valley evokes the multiple perceptions from the visible which still brings nature dear to us though such visible.

The serenity is still visible from certain points and grasping those moments from those locations evoke nature as human eyes could aestheticize for his sake. On the other hand, nature tries to retain as wild as it could be.

CONCLUSION

Art and Sexuality

Mahadeve temple, Teku, Kathmandu

Sexuality in art speaks both about sacred and profane, and more discursively blurs the distinction between profane and sacred. Nepali art of the valley not merely asks us to participate in understanding what sexuality is or displaces us from sexuality as in opposition to what divine and sacred are. Such double bind of the profane and sacred is pervasive in Indian and Nepali art. If, on the one hand, sexuality is associated with the union of knowledge and compassion, it is also the blissful bodily experience. In this section, my focus is to bring in multiple examples to elaborate my arguments.

Vajravarahi is one of the Matraka goddesses in Hindu tradition. She is recognized as Vajrayogini in Vajrayana Buddhist belief. She is the consort of Chakrasamvara, another god of Vajrayana tradition. The union of Chakrasamvara and Vajravarahi can be seen in many Nepali sculptures and paintings. Similar rhythmic embrace can be seen in the images of Kalachakra-Vishwamata, Samantabhadra-Samantabhadri, Achala-Aryachalnath and Biswabajri, Haivajra-Nairatmya, Hayagriva-Vajravarahi or Nairatma, Padmasambhava-

Yeshe Tsogyal (known as the mother of Tibet or Victorious ocean of wisdom in Tibetan language).

They are both sexual union in iconographic visuality and union of *Karuna* or compassion (male) and *Prajna* or wisdom (female). Furthermore, the union depicted in such images range in various notables: time and sky (in Kalachakra-Vishwamata), wrath and stillness (as in Achala-Aryachalnath) etc.

There are schools of thought which deny the idea of these images as the blatant union of sexual bodies. But sexual union has associations with the thought processes that go with the union of the body and mind. Sexuality and conceptual unions are not separate.

The greatest achievement of Chandella dynasty[14] was Khajuraho. There are constructions of some eighty-five temples. The temples are the masterpieces of art of the time. The tall temples are one of the most symmetrical structures seen in South Asia. On the temple walls there are elegant female figures and abundant sculptures and reliefs of provocative erotic sexual display of man and woman, and human and animal sexual acts. The major concentrations are of female figures and their exposed erotic bodies, more illustratively exposing their vulva. Khajuraho depicts even group sex, group of females with a single male. Along with the depiction of women supposedly of marginalized castes, there are scenes of drinking wine in human skulls as cups, eating and merry making, and also scenes of human sacrifice. Depiction of sex was common in the temples of that period. The Sun Temple are Konarak, Orissa has similar erotic carvings.

Why are there erotic carvings on the temples walls where within the temples there are images of gods and goddesses in sanctum sanctorum? Do the female nudes connote art? They certainly do

---

[14] Chandella Dynasty ruled Central India in the 11th century, the areas was present Madhyapradesh and Uttar Pradesh.

CONCLUSION

and how then abundant sex makes a temple the abode of the divine? How is the frame sex the structure is temple? Where is the dividing line between the profane and the sacred? Or is there no division at all? Does art celebrate the body as the site of the divine? How can both sex and sacred conjoin together?

The viewer goes through a series of sexual images of unconventional kind and encounters the goddess. The mundane is transformed immediately into divine. There is no division between outside and inside, external and internal. The aesthetic of pleasing the senses leads to the moral domain of the shrine. Sex is the form which does not bar but leads to the comprehension of the moral. The meaning of the pleasure and moral are evoked within a single stretch of walking out and in, and in and out.

The art maps first the bodies for the viewer, the very physical and the very place of desire, and then lets them realize the other of art, the ethics of the deity's presence. The frame is the site of meaning, where vital distinctions between inside and outside, between moral and immoral are created. The poet Kalidasa maps the body of the goddess to give the impression of a meditating being:

> The first clear rain-drop falling on her brow
> Gem it one moment of their light, and now
> Kissing her sweet lips find a welcome rest
> In the deep valley of the lady's breast.
> They wander broken by the fall within
> The mazy channels of her dimpled skin.
> Kalidasa in *Kumarasambhava*

The body corresponds to the meditating self. Art helps realize such visions. The sexual bodies are located in the realm of the divine not as profane, but in association with the divine. It is not merely about the common comprehension that sex is depicted as the symbolism of impure, sex is depicted as the association of the pure, so both are

Chinnmasta, the Goddess of Knowledge, Patan

CONCLUSION

pure, the impure is pure or the pure is impure. There then is no distinction between the good and bad. Binarism is dangerous. One may ask what pure is in impure. What is pure in pure? Doesn't pure need something external to make it pure, something that is distinct from the pure. Pure is not a necessary condition and sufficient in itself to mean what it means. As pure needs outside of itself to be meaningful, the impure too does. They are in need of one another. That very need probably is illustrated in the temple. The one complements the other. The art is completion of the secular. It challenges and even threatens the moral singularity of religion, the coded institutionalized religion, to be precise.

The sexual nude is the body balanced to reform the idea of the divine: the erotic is the fullness of providing meaning to the moral of religion, and it is done through art. Sex thus the necessary object of art. Art illustrates culture in the very esoteric mode. For instance, the sexual in art is un-viewable for many but is up there on the wall to be viewed. There is no voyeurism because the artists have not created the perspective of the keyhole. We construct keyholes in the openness, it is the psychology of the viewer. But the erotic is immediate, direct, bold, in front of the viewer and hence art is the confidence of creativity.

The temples in Kathmandu valley have such tradition of creativity which stuns conventional viewership. By the very site of the sexual, the sacred resides. The sexual is both sensuous and sensual. There is nothing hidden to the viewer, neither the sacred not the sexual.

"Why is it that I cannot observe the copulating deities?" asked Daman[15] who accompanied us to Bhaktapur just a month before Covid lockdown. Sexuality is not only about sex but the entire expressions, behaviors, ideas and attitudes we associate with sex

---

[15] I have changed the name of the student.

Mahadev Temple Teku, Kathmandu

from laws to politics, art to economism. Copulating bodies are forbidden public visibility and when art reveals the forbidden, the interpretive mind works from the law of the forbidden. Art is also what the system of forbiddance limits our imagination to profanity and profanity does not hold much ground to reveals the aspects of sacredness, or better yet there is nothing that can be conceptualized as profane and sacred. Art collapses any polarity of concepts and Nepali art does it with mythopoetic attitudes.

EPILOGUE
Art, Myth, and Anger

As an episodic end to the book, this chapter is a about one of the most significant emotions which have determined the contemporary times and its current course of history. It is anger. Anger has been a significant aspect of artistic expression. Anger also is the problem in terms with conflict, violence, oppression, but on the other hand, anger is also a necessary expression to right the wrong, to discipline, and to resist. Anger is multi-shaded: destructive, creative, aggressive, defensive, necessary, unnecessary, ideologized masculine, and violence against women. There are multiple conceptualizations of anger.

Oneness.

Myths have multiple expressions of anger. In Hindu mythical narratives, Durga's calm and sublime anger is how she delivers Mahisasura from sin to assimilation into divinity. Durga who defeats or rather assimilates the demon Mahishasura into her fold with a smile and meditative calm. It is not, I conceive, the killing of the demon by god but a mode of deliverance. But in the *Mahabharata*, Bhim's and Draupadi's anger are vengeance and satisfaction from the vengeance. Bhim tears apart the chest of his enemy brother Dushashana to fulfill the vow of his wife Draupadi to wet her hair by the enemy's blood. Narasimha the incarnation of Hindu god Vishnu descends to the earth to punish his arch enemy Hiranyakashipu. The god tears his flesh apart in front of his devotee Prahlad, the son of Hiranyakashipu. The god's anger is displayed in front of an adolescent in a most excruciating and traumatic moment: the killing of Prahlad's father by the fatherly god.

In Greek mythology, Athena is the goddess of wisdom. She curses Tiresias when he saw the deity and her friends bathing naked under a stream. You have seen too much, she fumes and curses him to be blind. The ignorant man pleads for forgiveness because he happened to see them and did not intended to watch them bathing. Athena forgives him in the most ironic mode. She blesses her to be able to see the future which was more a curse in disguise. Marsyas the flute player challenges Apollo in a musical contest and is defeated. Apollo flays him alive which he does with time and patience like an artist. The Renaissance painter Titian's "Flaying of Marsyas" depicts calm cruel Apollo while Orpheus plays the lira, perhaps a melancholic tone. An other case of pain and anger is related with Medusa. Medusa's anger against cruelty, viciousness is replete with agony. Medusa whose anger is the agony of her being the victim. In the arctic narratives from Finland, anger is expressed by assaulting the opponent in poems

EPILOGUE

> Angry then was Väinämöinen,
> Filled with wrath and indignation,
> And himself commenced his singing,
> And to speak his words of wisdom. (*Kalevala*[1])

The hero god of the Finnish epic *Kalevala*, Väinämöinen punishes Joukahainen with anger expressed by singing. Anger is the wrath of god who sings as he punishes and at the same time disseminates his wisdom.

Gandhi's non-violence against the British empire as the form of anger which can be understood as the political counterpart of Durga's calm anger of deliverance. The myth symbolically revisits as political, in the acts of Mahatma Gandhi[2].

Anger's abode is very near our tranquil mind. Anger and calmness live together. A change in situation and anger displays its tooth and claw and the serenity vaporizes. Amygdala in the brain pounds.

We may think that the twentieth century has been the age of anger, but twenty first century is no different than the crusading middle ages, neither the time of the Mongols nor that of the Victorians. What happened in Sobibor or Sarajevo is no different than the Pearl Harbor and the Atom bomb on the cities, and even the rat race of capitalism. From street violence to honor killing, misogyny, protecting cows by lynching others, religious persecution of the Rohingyas, colonialism, America first, nationalism to racism, anger is the most brutal emotion that pervades over all such ideas, attitudes, and actions.

---

[1] See *Kalevala: The Land of the Heroes*. Trans. W. F. Kirby. London: Everyman's Library, 1966 (Runo III, lines 283-286).

[2] The idea of anger came to me after making a documentary "Anger and the Mahatma" in 2022. Many of the ideas in this essays are my delivery as a host of the film.

A journalist in Hungry tripping a refugee parent with a baby who tumbles on the ground is as disturbing as lynching the black boy in the plantations in America. Naill Ferguson in his book *The War of the World* asks something like who ate the bodies in Auschwitz. We may think we all ate them, moral Europe and America, South Asians, we all devoured them. I always wonder how did the age of Europe sleep in the night when humanity was charred into the gas chambers? What moral leaders dreamt in the night when the whole world was witnessing Nelson Mandela in Robben Island? I was a college boy then and I always wondered how can he be in jail for twenty-seven long years for asking for liberation from the white colonizers? I always was angry, simply angry, not causing harm to anyone. And still to talk about anger is to be angry.

I have discussed in the chapter Mahadashami: the mystic smile in the act of killing" about the image of goddess Durga from Bhaktapur Durbar Square. She is a powerful Hindu mythological being. One can see that it is the moment of death blow by a deity of cosmic proportion to an equally powerful demon, Mahishasura. The goddess is piercing her lance into the chest of the evil incarnate.[3] Her anger disguised or is it the eternal smile of rage? Is she looking at a distance while killing the demon because the evil is insignificant? Why is she in a meditative detachment away from the target? Why is the target not targeted? The lance pierces the chest of the demon who looks helpless while she smiles looking elsewhere. What an engagement where the victor is not angry and the vanquished is not in terror but in a posture of compassionate sublime! Is he stupefied by the indifferent look of the goddess? The ultimate moment of death is the moment of union of the evil with the supernatural?

---

[3] As narrated in many Hindu narratives and more specially in the *Markandeya Purana*. The Puranas are the compendia of stories about creation, gods and goddesses, about morals, evils and the ways of the world.

EPILOGUE

How anger is displayed in this mythical image representing the narrative of the war of Durga and Mahishasura is a question which cuts across the idea of anger as does the political act of Gandhi against the British empire.

Let me come back to Medusa myth. Caravaggio's first version of Medusa's head was painted in 1596. Medusa is a mythical character from Greek mythology.

Do the hissing snakes of Medusa echo the pain of being raped? Medusa is the victim: god Poseidon had raped her inside the temple of the virgin goddess. Goddess Athena, as punishment, had transformed her face because she had defiled the sacred by being raped. Raped and transformed, the innocent was victimized twice at the same harrowing sequence. There was a rivalry between Athena and Medusa. Who was more beautiful? Medusa certainly was, as the narratives depict her. The fury-hissing is the memory of the past. Her aggression is revealed through serpent locks just after her head was severed.

Does her face justify the pain and anger of being raped, transformed, exiled, and murdered? Or is it too little an expression of rage because the sky does not fall upon Poseidon, Athena, and Perseus; Perseus who carries her head to protect himself from the enemies? If we do not know the story, we just read how one of the evil gorgons was killed by a hero, but when we do know, we know her unbearable pain inflicted on her body, hence her angry hissing face.

One of the supreme gods of Hindu mythology, Vishnu had to bear the perpetual hatred of Hiranyakashipu, Prahlad's father. Prahlad was Vishnu's devotee. Hiranyakashipu crosses the limits of hatred by punishing his son for being the follower of his arch enemy, the god. But the son was saved multiple times by Vishnu. Finally, Narasimha, the incarnation of Vishnu with the face of a loin and body of a man, descends to the earth to kill Hiranyakashipu. The demon king was formidable because he was blessed with immortality of not being killed by any living creature or non-living object, neither inside nor outside a residence, neither on the ground nor in the sky, and not by any weapon. The creator God Brahma had blessed him. Narasimha is part human, part animal and part divine, he chooses the twilight, chooses the threshold, puts him on his thighs, and not defying the boon, tears him by his nails and kills the evil incarnate.

The anger is the double bind of form. One is god's form which is none that exists as a living being, unique, only one that exists and seizes to exist after fulfilling the task, then the time which is in-between, the space which is neither in nor out, the nails which is neither a weapon nor not a weapon. The other form of anger is Vishnu who recreates its own law of nature dodging the law of Brahma, to kill the demon. Vishnu finds fissures, loopholes in Brahma's blessing of invincibility. But how is the anger with its terrible form impacts the mind of the little child? He stands praying, certainly terrified witnessing the death of his father in the most excruciating manner amidst unearthly and unheavenly roar of the victor and the unbearable pain of the victim, witnessing the father and his rescuer god the father, in the indeterminate time between darkness and light, like in a waking dream, in the moment of salvation in the very act of killing, in the motherless moment of masculinity. Does Prahlad thus celebrate the anger by his eternal sensibility of devotion? Does devotion overpower the act of killing his enemy father? Anger is the lack of anything sublime and yet it is the moment of salvation for the world. Is the anger necessary to free humankind of evil?

Mahatma Gandhi fought against the colonial power of global proportion. Were Gandhi's ideas and actions over the British empire anger? Is Satyagraha an expression of anger? If the anger was expressed to right the wrong, Gandhi was in this sense, angry[4]. Gandhian self-restrain and conscious suffering may have been the Bhaava called Aavega or agitation, performed on the real-life drama. The calm of the Mahatama of Satyagraha and Ahimsa had the underlying anxiety for freedom. Gandhi writes,

> When a person claims to be non-violent, he is expected not to be angry with one who has injured him. He will not wish him harm, he will wish him well … Non-violence is complete innocence.

Non-violence, for Gandhi, can be understood[5] in terms with the consequence of not being angry. He does not seem to say that non-violence is not anger. A non-violent person will not wish you harm but will wish you well. Instead of what non-violence is, Gandhi is talking about the expectation and wish from a non-violent person. Since the actor does not harm the acted upon, it is the force of the will to be innocent and calm. Gandhi's force of non-violence with the goal of freedom is the political counterpart of goddess Durga's meditative calm. Gandhi's political will cuts deep into the idea of anger as transformation into self-sacrifice. Anger does not disappear but is transformed as emancipatory force of the will. This is where anger is tamed to the creative act of liberation.

---

[4] As James R. Averill, an expert in the field of emotion studies may define Gandhi's emotion as anger. Averill thinks, "Anger refers to an emotional state that involves both an attribution of blame for some perceived wrong and an impulse to correct the wrong or prevent its recurrence" (Pahlavan 4). See Pahlavan, Farzaneh. Ed. *Multiple Facets of Anger: Getting Mad or Restoring Justice*. New York: Nova, 2011.

[5] Gerber, William. (1967). (Ed.). *The Mind of India*. London: Southern Illinois University Press.

The Mahatma had the creative dynamics of anger within the calm.

Gandhi's favorite song "Vaishnav jana to tine kahiye jo peer parayi jane re!" speaks about Vaishanav being those who can internalize the pains of others. His anger may have been expressed by such internalization of millions suppressed under the British rule.

Humanism is anthropomorphic anger of superiority. Genocide is anger towards humans. Progress is anger toward the earth. Patriarchy is anger against the body of women. Nationalism is anger of claiming singularity. Hospitality is territorial anger of arrogance in disguise against migrating wanderers: see we welcome the unwelcomable in our domain. But a wise man says, hospitality rests outside it, the guest permits you to be hospitable; you host because of the guest[6].

Shantideva in "Perfection of Patience" in *Boddhisttavas's Way of Life* writes:

> ... one should earnestly cultivate patience in various ways. The mind does not find peace, nor does it enjoy pleasure and joy, nor does it find sleep or fortitude when the thorn of hatred dwells in the heart.
>
> Even dependents whom one rewards with wealth and honors wish to harm the master who is repugnant due to his anger.

---

[6] See Jacques Derrida's concept of hospitality in many of his works.

BIBLIOGRAPHY OF WORK CITED

Bart Dessein. (1999). "Introduction" in Bart Dessein. ed. *The Notion of Self in Buddhism Communication and Cognition.* Vol 32, No 1/2.

Bhattacharya, Binoytosh. (1958). *The Indian Buddhist Iconography.* Calcutta: Farma K L Mukhopadhyaya.

Bhattacharya, Gaurishwar. "Iconography of Stone Sculptures." https://www.academia.edu/38775320/2018_ICONOGRAPHY_OF_STONE_SCULPTURES

Bileu, Max. (1996). "The Mytho-Poetic Attitude" in Pierre Brunel. *Companion to Literary Myths, Heroes, and Archetypes*: 1996: 863)

Carl, Jung. (1977 print) *The Archetypes and the Collective Unconscious* in The Collected Works of C. G. Jung. Volume 9, Part 1. Ed. Sir Herbert Read et al. Trans. R. F. C. Hull. Princeton: Princeton UP.

———. (1964). *Man and His Symbols.* London: Penguin Arkana.

Doniger, Wendy. Ed. Trans & Annotations. (1981). *Rig Vida, an Anthology.* London: Penguin.

Eiseley, Loren. (2009). "How Flowers Changed the World" in Richard Dawkins. (Ed.). *The Oxford Book of Modern Science Writing.* New York.

Girard, René. (2005). *Violence and the Sacred.* London: Continuum.

Goudriaan, Teun & Sanjukta Gupta. (1981). Ed. Jan Gonda. *A History of Indian Literature: Hindu Tantric and Sakta Literature.* Vol II. Wiesbaden: Otto Harrassowitz.

Gupto, Arun. (2018). *Goddesses of Kathmandu Valley: Grace, Rage, Knowledge.* 2nd Ed. London: Routledge.

———. (2021). *Anger and the Mahatma.* Producer. Soma Gupta.

Hume, R. E. (1998). *The thirteen principle Upanishads.* New Delhi: Oxford UP.

Kalidas. *The Birth of the War-God* or *Kumarsambhava.* Trans. Ralph T. H. Griffith. (2010) Guttenberg Ebook, Release Date: April 12, 2010 [EBook #31968]

Kemmerer, Lisa. 2006. *In Search of Consistency: Ethics and Animals.* Leiden: Brill.*Krishna: The Beautiful Legend of God: Srimad Bhagavata Purana (Bk.10).* Trans. Edwin Bryant. London: Penguin Books, 2003)

Moyers, Bill. (1991). *The Power of Myth: Joseph Campbell with Bill Moyers.* New York: First Anchor Books Edition.

Mukherjee, Radhakamal. (1984). *The Culture and Art of India.* New Delhi: Munshiram Manoharlal.

Nagar, Shantilal. (1998). *Indian Gods and Goddesses: The Early Deities from Chalcolithic to Beginning of Historical Period.* Vol. 1. Delhi: B.R. Publishing Corporation. Nepali, Gopal Singh. (2015). *The Newars: An Ethno-Sociological Study of a Himalayan Community.* Kathmandu: Mandala.

Nepali, Gopal Singh. (2015). *The Newars.* Kathmandu, Mandala Book Point.

Pargitar, Eden F. (1904). *The Markandeya Purana.* Calcutta: The Asiatic Society.

Rust, Frances. (1969). *Dance in Society: An Analysis of the Relationship between the Social Dance and Society in England from the Middle Ages to the Present.* Oxon: Routledge.

Samuel, G. (2008). *The origins of yoga and tantra: Indic religions to the thirteenth century.* Cambridge, UK: Cambridge University Press

Sangari, Kumkum & Sudesh Vaid. (2006). (Eds.). *Recasting Women: Essays in Colonial History.* New Delhi, Zubaan.

Sastri, Panditabhushana V. Subramanhaya. Trans. (1946). *Varahamihira's Brihat Samhita*. Bangalore: V.B. Soobbiah & Sons. https://archive.org/details/Brihatsamhita/mode/2up

'Shravak', Lalji. (1999). "Buddha's Rejection of the Brahmanical Rejection of Atman" in Bart Dessein. ed. *The Notion of Self in Buddhism Communication and Cognition*. Vol 32, No 1/2.

Shakya, Min Bahadur. (1994). *The Iconography of Nepalese Buddhism*. Kathmandu: Buddha Dharma Education Association. Inc. www.buddhanet.net

Shakya, Milan Ratna. (2017). *Maṇḍala of Nepāla Maṇḍala: Buddhist Arts and Cultural Tradition of Kathmandu Valley*. New Delhi: Aadarsh Book.

Spivak, Gayatri Chkarvorty. (2012). *An Aesthetic Education in the Era of Globalization*. Cambridge: Harvard UP.

Yeatman, Anna. (1997). "The Place of Women's Studies in the Contemporary University" in *Feminisms*. Eds. Sandra Kemp & Judith Squires. Oxford: OUP.

Nebesky-Wojkowitz, René De. (1996). *Oracles and Demons of Tibet: The Cult of Iconography of the Tibetan Protective Deities*. Delhi: Book Faith India.

Zimmer, Heinrich. (1965). *Myths and Symbols in Indian Art and Civilization*. New York: Harper Torchbooks.

INDEX

Aesthetics 7, 82, 104
Anger 110, 111, 125, 127, 130, 131, 134, 142
Animal xi, 69
Art 119, 121, 123–125, 134, 135, 142

Buddha 7, 27, 28, 69, 74, 75, 104, 105, 107, 108, 113–118, 135
Buddhist 7, 12–14, 21, 24, 26, 27, 35, 65, 66, 74, 75, 77, 79, 93, 96, 108, 109, 115, 119

City 1, 10, 31, 43, 142
consciousness 4, 14, 15, 19, 32, 48, 51, 76, 101–103, 107, 108
Cow 72

Death 8, 70, 71, 76, 79
Demon 64
Durga 21, 24, 27, 28, 35, 43, 61–68, 110, 126–129, 131

Form 104

Ganesh 24, 25, 106
God 25, 71, 83, 130, 134
Goddess 17, 28, 63, 66–68, 79, 122, 129

Hindu 4, 6, 7, 11–14, 17, 21, 22, 24, 25, 27, 32, 34–36, 39, 40, 46, 48, 55, 64, 70–75, 77–79, 82, 84, 86, 89, 90, 93, 95, 96, 107, 109, 110, 119, 126, 128, 129

Iconography 90, 113
Indra 25, 53, 54, 55, 57, 58, 59

Killing 28, 61, 63, 101
Knowledge 67, 122, 134, 142
Krishna 17, 24, 31–37, 65, 73, 112, 134

Lakhe 25, 27

Mandala 2, 76, 77, 107, 108, 117, 118, 134
Myth 4–6, 11, 31, 101, 102, 125, 134
Mythopoetic 1

Nature 3, 77
Parvati 24, 43, 47, 62

Religion 56
Ritual 40, 72

Sacred 32, 46, 61, 115

Sacrifice 58
Season 7
Self 69, 75, 77
Sex 82, 121, 123
Sexuality 119, 120, 123
Shiva 12, 17, 24, 35, 43, 47, 55, 65, 68, 79, 84
Snake 14, 17
Symbolism 82, 107

Tantra 25, 33–35

Urban 10

Vishnu 12, 13, 17, 24, 36, 37, 67, 73, 84, 126, 129, 130

Woman 50